AMPLIFYING IMPACT

AMPLIFYING IMPACT

UNLOCKING INNOVATION, EQUITY, AND CAPACITY IN NONPROFITS

HARRISON G. HOLCOMB

NEW DEGREE PRESS
COPYRIGHT © 2022 HARRISON G. HOLCOMB
All rights reserved.

AMPLIFYING IMPACT
Unlocking Innovation, Equity, and Capacity in Nonprofits

ISBN   979-8-88504-085-3 *Paperback*
        979-8-88504-714-2 *Kindle Ebook*
        979-8-88504-193-5 *Ebook*

Dedication

This book is dedicated to my parents: Greg and Jennifer Holcomb.

Thank you for supporting my commitment to building a better world.

CONTENTS

	INTRODUCTION	**9**
	PART 1	**17**
CHAPTER 1.	HOW DID WE GET HERE? NONPROFIT HISTORY IN THE UNITED STATES	19
CHAPTER 2.	FOLLOW THE MONEY: HOW NONPROFIT FUNDING PRACTICES SHAPE THE SECTOR	25
CHAPTER 3.	TRUST—IT'S COMPLICATED	51
	PART 2	**63**
CHAPTER 4.	HIGH STAKES PHILANTHROPY: THE RISKS AND REWARDS OF MASSIVE GIFTS	65
CHAPTER 5.	INCLUSION AND INCENTIVES: THE POWER OF NONPROFIT BOARDS	79
CHAPTER 6.	NONPROFITS AND GOVERNMENT: MOVING FROM PASSIVE TO PARTNER	95
	PART 3	**105**
CHAPTER 7.	THE SPECIAL RELATIONSHIP: CONNECTIONS BETWEEN DONORS AND NONPROFITS	107
CHAPTER 8.	TRUST BUT VERIFY: A CASE FOR A NONPROFIT ACCREDITATION MODEL	121

CHAPTER 9.	ELEMENTS OF A SECTOR-WIDE ACCREDITATION SYSTEM	133
CHAPTER 10.	PUTTING ACCREDITATION INTO PRACTICE	151
	CONCLUSION	**165**
	ACKNOWLEDGMENTS	**169**
	APPENDIX	**171**

Introduction

My career in nonprofits began with a painfully early commute on a damp, gray January morning in Washington, DC. Nursing a slight hangover from start-of-semester festivities over the weekend, I rode two buses and the metro to a converted nineteenth century convent tucked away at the end of an alley in Chinatown. The building was Dickensian with narrow windows, peeling paint, and a hodgepodge of secondhand furniture spanning at least a century. I was a junior in college, studying public health, and this building was to be my base of operations. It contained a transitional housing facility for women, operated by a large nonprofit in the city, where I had been assigned to spend the semester completing a community-based internship. Although I didn't know it at the time, it was also going to be the site of a central decision point in my life and career.

I always imagined I would work in nonprofits or government. But, until this internship, I had very little practical experience in either sector. I had done the obligatory tutoring and community service projects for the National Honor Society and Beta Club in high school. However, this internship was to be a crash course in how nonprofits operated. The twelve weeks passed quickly and informatively. I am sincerely grateful for that overworked team, in the converted nuns' cells they used for offices. They taught me how to write a grant, introduced me to resourceful, tenacious professionals and residents, and were endlessly patient with my questions.

I enjoyed my time there, more than any of my later internships on Capitol Hill or at a consulting firm. It felt immediate, purposeful, and connected, unlike the preparation of slick slide decks or painstaking updates to constituent databases. True, work at nonprofits was distinctly unglamorous, with low pay, old computers, and even older chairs. But the needs and pain of people experiencing homelessness felt raw, immediate, and intense. Time spent listening to their stories, providing assistance, championing investment, and supporting their journeys felt impactful and important, in a way that even the most elegant policy analysis whitepaper, prepared and sold to USAID, just didn't. Combine that sense of urgency and impact with the grant-writing and research skills that got me my first job out of college, and my career as one of tens of millions of nonprofit professionals in the United States was launched.

Nonprofits, like the homeless services agency where I interned, have a long history as part of civil society. Building on traditions of community solidarity and charitable giving that predate the founding of the United States, many cities and towns had free schools, food, and shelter aid for the poor and indigent, and various forms of public art, all provided by contributions from citizens as early as the seventeenth century (Arnsberger et. al, 2008). However, nonprofits only gained a formal legal structure and the all-important tax-exemption in the late nineteenth century when a series of new laws began to reshape the federal tax system (ibid).

Building on this tradition, the sector, in the twenty-first century, has become an essential but often invisible weft in the social fabric in the United States. We rely on nonprofits to fill critical roles. Approximately 1.6 million 501(c)(3) tax exempt public charities in the US fill countless needs, from healthcare services like hospitals and nursing homes to supporting symphonies and museums (Independent Sector, 2021). Other types of nonprofit organizations like churches, synagogues, and mosques tend to the spiritual lives of millions of Americans, and 501(c)(4) advocacy organizations play an influential role in civil society.

In many cities, including my current home Denver, nonprofits are the largest providers of healthcare services, homeless services, and supplemental food, from prepared meals for seniors to food pantries for families. But the reach of nonprofits goes far beyond the safety net. Even if they don't realize it, most Americans interact with a nonprofit daily. Whether it is the PTA at their child's school, their doctor's office, or walking through a park, chances are good that the donors, volunteers, and staff of a tax-exempt organization were behind it.

Beyond their programming, nonprofit organizations are major employers and economic engines. Johns Hopkins University researchers analyzing the labor force in the United States estimate that over 12.5 million people are employed by nonprofits, collectively bringing home more than $680 billion in earnings. In terms of total employees, the nonprofit sector is more than double the size of the transportation industry, including massive airlines like American, Delta, or Southwest, and a third larger than the professional services industry and its behemoths like Deloitte or Ernst and Young. As noted in a report on giving statistics compiled by Charity Navigator, private charitable donations have consistently been 2–3 percent of US gross domestic product in any given year since the 1970s. In fact, Giving USA's analysis found that, in 2019, at least $449 billion dollars were contributed to 501(c)(3)s alone.

Given its scale, breadth, and the essential nature of the services it provides, the effective functioning of the nonprofit sector has a profound impact on the nation. Dysfunction at a high-profile company providing a beloved convenience like ridesharing or food delivery can be disruptive and annoying. But dysfunction at an organization like the Red Cross, which forms an essential backbone of disaster response following floods, fires, and tornadoes, is nothing short of catastrophic.

Unsurprisingly, there is a lot of discourse about the sector. You can find commentary and research on the nonprofit sector in almost every medium from Tik-Tok to hardback books. Much like other industries, the conversation about nonprofits happens in two broad silos: one for the "insiders," mostly nonprofit professionals, and one for everybody else. Insiders tend to read specialized publications and newsletters and congregate in closed LinkedIn groups or invite-only conferences. Insiders have their distinctive jargon, jokes, tropes, and stereotypes.

Outsiders probably don't hear much about the nonprofit sector. Beyond the occasional glamorous photo from an extravagant charity gala on Instagram or an embezzlement scandal (which are the main clickbait), most may only think about nonprofits at tax time. When more in-depth content about nonprofits filters out to the wider world, it tends to be created by outsiders: journalists, academics, or salespeople trying to persuade you to open a Donor Advised Fund. When nonprofit professionals do address the wider community, there is almost always an ask— for you to text your congressman, dump ice water on your head, run a 5k, or write a check.

The conversation among outsiders about nonprofits is often focused on questions of money. The dialogue centers on which organizations to support and which might be overpaying their CEOs. Further, conversation also almost always happens between outsiders. Donors consult financial advisors; financial advisors consult academic researchers. Rarely does anyone bother to directly query the nonprofit organizations they are discussing.

Dividing information about nonprofits into silos for insiders and outsiders has consequences. As a nonprofit professional who raises money, I straddle both silos, spending time with donors, philanthropic advisors, and for-profit consultants in addition to my colleagues in the field. This has given me insight into how the information disconnect between the two groups creates confusion, builds mistrust, and erodes mutual respect. The isolation between the two groups means that the shared vocabulary, data, and skills needed for mutual understanding are missing. The fact that many of the insiders who do communicate widely outside the sector are often doing so to collect money, time, or attention only compounds this mistrust.

I hope to use this book to begin to break down these silos and open a more frank and fully informed dialogue between donors, volunteers, concerned citizens, and the millions of passionate, skilled professionals inside the nonprofit sector. A thriving nonprofit sector is essential to building a thriving society. Only through mutual trust and open conversation can we hope to reach that goal. In the face of complex challenges like systemic racism, wealth inequality, and environmental sustainability, we cannot operate in silos. As the immediacy of these challenges have manifested in compounding crises across the United States, we have seen plenty of acts of personal and organizational heroism. We have also seen parts of the nonprofit sector stressed to the breaking point. Resilience in the face of difficult and uncertain times requires mutual understanding of the strengths and weaknesses of the sector and a clear conception of its needs and opportunities.

In this book, by sharing my experiences and curating the insight and wisdom of others who have generously shared with me, I aim to be a small part of that much larger dialogue. I am not the only, or the most authoritative, expert on the nonprofit sector. My perspective is shaped by the privilege I carry in society as a white, cis male from a middle-class background. However, I offer a sincere and enduring commitment to the power and value of the nonprofit sector in creating a stable, just, and vibrant society. Ever since I first perched on a creaking antique chair for orientation at the transitional shelter in Washington, DC, I have been a believer in the power of the nonprofit sector to build a more just world. In the years since that day, I have been fortunate to accumulate more than a decade of lived experience working in a range of nonprofits large and small with diverse missions, complemented with continuing education, fellowships, and volunteering. Finally, I bring authenticity and honesty. I am not writing on behalf of any organization, nor am I trying to curry favor with anyone. This book will offer the most direct analysis and unvarnished insights I can offer.

In the coming chapters, I sketch out the nonprofit sector and its key relationships with beneficiaries, donors, and government. This picture is shaded in areas where there is misalignment and misunderstanding. But there are also many bright places where innovation, cooperation, and harmony are creating great outcomes. Some of these areas are structural in nature, many of them focus on incentives, and a few are simply driven by human nature. I also aim to offer a perspective on where we might go together, collectively as insiders and outsiders alike, from here, with a goal to build on the sector's strengths, address its weaknesses, and better ensure open, respectful relationships between stakeholders.

I hope that the content is engaging to all stakeholders in the nonprofit sector. For donors and volunteers, I offer greater insight into the true challenges, opportunities, and needs of the sector. For those who work in nonprofits, I offer inspiration to invite more open, honest conversations within the sector and with donors and outsiders. Finally, for policy makers, I humbly offer insights about how the government can facilitate the success and effectiveness of nonprofits as a critical economic engine for the United States.

Both deeply rooted in tradition and remarkably light and flexible in their legal framework, nonprofit organizations play a unique and expansive role in the life of the United States. Their work touches the lives of tens of millions of citizens every day, whether as an employer, as an essential rope in the safety net, or by enriching their communities. As the United States faces greater pressure from compounding challenges like climate change, pandemic disease, racial injustice, and wealth inequality, nonprofits are likely to play an even more outsized role in the social fabric of the nation.

However, nonprofits face many challenges—some mirroring larger social struggles for justice and equity, others unique to their special role. These challenges are magnified by silos in discourse about the nonprofit sector, reinforcing mistrust and misunderstanding. This book is intended to break down those silos by offering an authentic, transparent assessment of the state of the sector and recommendations for its future from a sincerely committed nonprofit insider.

PART 1

CHAPTER 1

How Did We Get Here? Nonprofit History in the United States

―

When I stepped into the converted Carmelite convent in Washington, DC, I was stepping into centuries of tradition. Nonprofits have a long history as a part of civil society in North America and have come to play a distinctive role in how we organize our communities. Understanding this story of moral aspirations, practical considerations, and human desires is essential to understanding the nonprofit sector.

The modern nonprofit sector has its roots in traditions of community support and religious traditions of charitable giving that predate the establishment of the United States. Even under British rule, many cities and towns had free schools, food, and shelter aid for the poor and indigent, and various forms of public art have been provided by contributions from citizens as early as the seventeenth century. Notable examples of this include Harvard University and the

College of William and Mary established in 1636 and 1696 respectively (Arnsberger 2008). During the Civil War, charitable organizations, particularly religious groups including the Society of Friends (Quakers) and Catholic monastic orders like the Daughters of Charity, played a critical role in operating hospitals to care for sick and wounded soldiers (Rada 2014).

These activities, while large in scale and critically important to the social fabric, were largely the province of religious and informal community groups. This meant that the organizations and the services they provided lacked any clear structure to give them independent support. It also means that people who chose to support them did so, not for any tax incentive or benefit, but out of self-interest, spiritual concern, or a desire for community recognition.

Thus, from their earliest days, nonprofits have been built on multiple foundations. On the one hand, they have been created to manifest spiritual or moral goals, like the Christian concept of charity. On the other hand, they have often represented a pragmatic solution to mundane problems in communities. The third foundational element is the desire to preserve and transmit social and cultural capital, through activities like education or artistic creation.

The real shifts that embedded and formalized nonprofits as official, distinct structures with a legal identity in the United States came in the late nineteenth and early twentieth centuries. In response to the growing wealth disparities associated with the so-called "gilded age," significant changes were made to the tax code. During this period a series of new laws influenced the reshaping of the taxation system at the federal and state levels—most notably, creating corporate and income taxes. These changes in systems of taxation created the opportunity to design new structures for organizing and financing the work of charitable institutions.

Two of the laws that were important in establishing the nonprofit sector as we know it today are: the Wilson-Gorman Tariff Act of 1894, which established a tax exemption for charitable organizations; and the Revenue Act of 1917, which established an income tax deduction for contributions to tax-exempt organizations. These two pieces of legislation created the framework for a tax-exempt corporation, the nonprofit, and a significant mechanism to ensure a clear incentive, beyond a moral imperative for individuals to make charitable donations. That incentive to give, of course, is the opportunity for an income tax deduction. In simplest terms, this policy allows individuals to deduct contributions made to certain tax-exempt organizations, including 501(c)(3) nonprofits, from their taxable income. Thus, individuals could choose to direct their money toward causes of their choosing and in turn pay less in taxes for the federal government to distribute as it sees fit.

Additional legislation in 1950 and 1969 further defined the operating criteria for tax-exempt organizations and limits on their activities. Since then, the legal framework for the sector has remained relatively unchanged (Arnsberger 2008). This includes the proportion of dollars that Americans contribute to charity under tax-exemption rules, which as noted by The Giving Institute in their *Insights* blog, has hovered at about 2 percent of GDP for much of the post-WWII era.

However, despite the flat rate of philanthropic giving, the role of nonprofits in keeping society functioning has continued to expand. A key driver in this expansion has been the evolving role of government. As noted by public administration researchers H. Brinton Milward and Keith Provan in their seminal paper on the topic, *Governing the Hollow State*, governments at all levels in the United States have increasingly chosen to outsource an ever-increasing array of services and processes. Frequently, those services are outsourced to nonprofits, a phenomenon they label as the "hollow state." The result is that more government funding flows into nonprofits, and nonprofits are increasingly involved in administering programs that were historically the province of government. This also means that the volume of government funds flowing in the form of contracts has increased.

The history of nonprofits in the United States touches on deep cultural, legal, and social traditions. It has often involved balancing pragmatic concerns, social troubles, and moral aspirations. With shifts in how government provides service in the twenty-first century, the nonprofit sector has become an essential but often invisible part of the social fabric in the United States. We rely on nonprofit organizations to fill so many critical roles, including ensuring that low-income and vulnerable Americans' basic needs are met.

The approximately 1.6 million 501(c)(3) tax-exempt public charities operating in the US provide essential services, from healthcare in hospitals and nursing homes, to enriching cultural life by supporting symphonies, theater companies, and museums (Independent Sector 2021). As noted by the National Council of Nonprofits, they often do so with very modest resources, given that over 90 percent of those organizations serve those needs with annual revenue of $1 million or less. Historically, and in the present day, the nonprofit sector is very much a community-based, grassroots network, a few giant organizations notwithstanding.

Understanding this history and present reality is essential to understanding the tensions and challenges that characterize the modern nonprofit sector. Connecting to this rich past is also essential to envisioning a thriving future for the sector.

CHAPTER 2

Follow the Money: How Nonprofit Funding Practices Shape the Sector

―

The cream-colored envelope from the Dorothea Haus Ross Foundation was practically burning a hole in my pocket as I walked the four sticky blocks back to the office through an oppressively humid Durham summer afternoon. This hand-addressed envelope contained the agreement for the first grant I had secured at my first job out of college. The grant was for $35,000, and I was incredibly excited that the hours of (unpaid) work I had done researching potential foundations, identifying this one, reviewing its submission cycle and requirements, and crafting a letter of inquiry and full grant proposal that complied with those requirements had paid off. On a personal level, succeeding in securing this funding was a critical stepping-stone in my transition from unpaid intern to paid staff member at the organization, and once the agreement was safely stored in our (donated) office, I treated myself to a cupcake from the excellent Ninth Street Bakery.

More importantly, at our grassroots, international development organization, $35,000 would go a long way toward expanding and improving the facilities of Casa Materna, a "maternal waiting home" where pregnant people could stay close to the health clinic as they approached their due dates. It was a critical, low-cost tool for helping pregnant people to have safer deliveries. This was doubly true in this community with its poor or nonexistent roads and lack of cars. It offered decent meals, a safe place to stay, and, most importantly, access to healthcare for labor and delivery. Succeeding in raising those funds was exciting, as this project was something the community's leaders had been hoping to finance for a long time. It was also going to significantly expand our operating budget and, if we were successful, open the door for other funding to support our goals around improving access to quality healthcare in the community.

However, the Ross Foundation grant also represented a shift in how the organization was funded. For much of the group's history, it had depended on earned revenue from selling coffee and handicrafts supplemented with modest gifts from individuals. In general, the operating budget was raised a few thousand dollars at a time. Receiving this larger tranche of funds was helpful, as it allowed us to confidently make a commitment to a project that the community both wanted and needed. However, it also required us to shift our priorities. To fulfill the terms of the grant, this project had to become the primary focus for our small staff.

Additionally, the grant didn't include nearly enough dollars to cover the staff time associated with managing complicated international procurement processes, tracking the budget, and completing project reports to provide required updates to the foundation. Fortunately, the latter requirements were at least manageable, and the foundation was flexible and responsive when we needed a no-cost extension to the project to work out a customs dispute for certain supplies. I vividly remember the early mornings, late nights, and countless carefully drafted emails and rehearsed phone calls that it took to keep this project moving forward and compliant.

Upon reflection, my introduction to grantmaking and organizational budgeting at this grassroots nonprofit provided a clear case study of the complex and often challenging world of nonprofit finances. Many, if not most, nonprofit leaders are asked to balance the execution of long-term projects with meeting emergent community needs. They are asked to do this while relying on multiple, unstable funding streams, each with different purposes, reporting requirements, and timelines. The complexity and diversity of revenue streams that finance most nonprofits are one of the things that make them distinct from their for-profit and government peers.

Although for-profits must navigate complex market conditions, fundamentally their revenue comes from selling goods and services on an open market. For-profit management teams also have broad discretion to decide how to use their revenue. They can choose between investing in infrastructure, employee bonuses, shareholder dividends, or new product development as they see fit.

Similarly, governmental revenue, while subject to some variability, is much more predictable and tightly modeled. Each year the government, through well-defined legislative and administrative processes, gets to decide how to spend tax revenue. In contrast, nonprofits face a much more fragmented, complex, and restrictive set of revenue streams. This requires them to balance many competing priorities, constituent types, and professional skill sets to find success.

UNDERSTANDING NONPROFIT REVENUE STREAMS

Understanding how nonprofit financing differs from for-profit companies or government entities can seem esoteric. However, it is supremely important. Since nonprofits touch almost every American's life, understanding a bit more about their finances can enhance their relationship to those nonprofits in three critical ways. First, understanding financial incentives is key to understanding operating decisions made at nonprofits. Second, if you are a donor or taxpayer, it is valuable context in trying to make good decisions about financially supporting nonprofits. Third, transparency builds trust. To break down this complex topic, this chapter will first describe nonprofit revenue, then explore expenses and debt financing, and finally outline some tips and principles for making sense of it all as a consumer, donor, or concerned citizen. Providing a high-level overview of these topics is intended to help elucidate key ideas and general principles.

Nonprofit revenue comes from four broad categories: earned income, government contracts or other public funding, philanthropic support, and investment income. Each of these revenue streams comes with its own set of advantages, challenges, and restrictions that a nonprofit must consider in determining which revenues to pursue in support of its mission.

EARNED INCOME

By sheer volume, earned revenue is the largest source of income for the nonprofit sector. According to the National Center for Charitable Statistics at the Urban Institute, earned revenue from programs, including fulfilling government contracts, represented almost three-fourths of nonprofit revenues in 2019, with charitable gifts, grants, and events making up the remainder. This figure is likely heavily skewed by the very large volumes of earned income generated by a small number of large nonprofits. Health systems, universities, or elite performing arts venues can all generate hundreds of millions of dollars of earned income annually.

However, it is very common for nonprofits of diverse sizes and missions to have some earned income as part of their revenue budgets. This revenue can come in many forms: student tuition, licensing of intellectual property, ticket sales, or item sales. The wrapping paper sale at your local PTA is a form of earned income. So is the admission ticket at a museum or the bill from a nonprofit health system.

One important benefit of earned revenue is that it is almost always unrestricted, giving the organization the flexibility to decide where and how to spend it. It can also help to expand an organization's base of support. Sales can bring new or different constituents into contact with the group as clients of the business. Finally, the money can be raised on the organization's timeline and terms, and there is plenty of room for creativity.

Beyond the unpredictability of competing for dollars in the marketplace, one of the most significant risks associated with earned income is mission creep. If an organization focuses too heavily on earning revenue, it may choose to prioritize the "business" over the purpose. Although such an approach might create short-term gains, it is bad for the organization in the long run, since it is likely to alienate other stakeholders and erode trust. Nonprofits are intended to serve specific types of missions, and the perception that earning revenue is the priority is very damaging. It could even lead to legal and tax issues. As outlined in Publication 598, the IRS can require nonprofits to pay taxes on "unrelated business income" if the organization is regularly carrying on a substantial earned income operation that is not substantively connected to the organization's exempt purpose.

This unrelated business income restriction in the tax code highlights another limitation of earned revenue; some organizational missions make it much easier to earn money this way. Organizations that focus on providing community services, like education or healthcare, have a much easier time earning revenue without running afoul of the unrelated business income restrictions. By contrast, organizations that focus on serving very low-income communities, or missions without an obvious client that can pay, like environmental protection groups, often struggle to find sources of earned income that can be considered substantially related to their core mission.

GOVERNMENT FUNDING

Government funding, in the form of contracts or grants, can be a great stabilizing revenue source for nonprofits. Government funding is particularly relevant to those with missions that align with common government services, for example food and nutrition programs or other basic services. Three positive features of government funding, from the nonprofit perspective, include accessibility, stability, and volume. This type of funding tends to be more accessible, as governments in the United States generally must follow open, transparent procurement processes that spell out exactly who can be funded, how funding decisions will be made, and the timeline.

This is only seldom the case for earned revenue or philanthropic giving. Government funding also tends to be more stable, as the basic priorities of government remain comparatively fixed, with more minor adjustments due to changing administrations or other factors. Also, the timing of changes in government priorities tends to be more predictable. Finally, the government has substantial resources, making grants or setting up contracts that only very few private individuals can match in terms of size.

One of the biggest drawbacks of government funding is that governments at all levels operate more slowly than other types of funders. They are notoriously slow to make payments to recipient organizations, which can create significant cash flow challenges for nonprofit organizations. Organizations that are heavily dependent on this revenue stream may even end up needing to take out loans to cover long waits for payments. For example, in New York City in 2019, an analysis found that the city owed nonprofits an estimated $744 million in back payments associated with grants and contracts, as organizations waited on average 282 days for a contract to be registered and payment to be issued.

The COVID-19 pandemic only exacerbated issues, as state and local governments faced plunging revenues and chaotic operations. In fact, in 2020, then-Governor Andrew Cuomo of New York issued an executive order suspending enforcement of the state's prompt payment laws for state contracts. Although some of these emergency measures have now been relaxed, in my experience, there is always some reason that payments are incomplete or behind schedule.

PHILANTHROPY

Philanthropic revenue is the third revenue stream that most nonprofits pursue. The biggest chunk of philanthropic revenue, about 80 percent in most years according to an analysis published in the *Insights* blog at Giving USA, comes from individual donors followed by foundations and for-profit corporate giving. Philanthropic revenue is one of the big wild cards among income streams for a nonprofit, since the individuals or organizations who make the gifts have extremely broad discretion to be flexible or rigid in restrictions, to make short- or long-term gifts, and to choose the size of their gift. It is also worth noting that, although the IRS doesn't assign it a monetary value for tax purposes, donated time and talent are an important part of philanthropic giving and can be a very difficult benefit to replace. For example, volunteers with specialized expertise may be essential to a particular nonprofit's mission and difficult to replace or acquire by other means.

Organizations seeking philanthropic revenue face the challenges of a shrinking number of donors and a stagnant number of dollars available, leading to intense competition. This intense competition, in turn, favors an ongoing arms race to develop the most compelling pitches, sophisticated analytics, and bespoke stewardship to lure donors. These strategies are expensive, require specialized skills, and can be labor intensive to execute. This creates a catch-22. In addition, the pursuit of private philanthropic dollars can create knotty ethical challenges for nonprofits. Should they accept dollars earned through activities that contribute to the problems they aim to solve? What about gifts from organizations that might be broadly engaged in unethical behavior even if it isn't specific to the particular mission of the nonprofit concerned? Additionally, much like government contracts, private philanthropy can come with restrictions on use of funds, complex reporting processes, and limited guarantees of timely payment.

INVESTMENT INCOME AND INTEREST

The final revenue stream common among nonprofits is more passive income, like interest from bank accounts and earnings from investments. A classic example of this is the university endowment, which is a big bolus of money that is invested strategically with the goal of generating both dividends and growth in value to fund operations at the school over a long period of time. In practice, for most nonprofits, this might look like earnings from a savings account with cash reserves, or perhaps the investment of a strategic reserve fund. The best thing about this revenue stream is that it generally requires comparatively little staff time and effort to realize. This type of income is also relatively predictable, particularly when considered over longer time horizons. Finally, this type of revenue stream, if well managed, can be tapped over very long periods of time, making it ideal for supporting core operations of an organization.

Because of the nature of how they are established and operated, it is worth noting that investment or endowment income at any meaningful scale is not accessible to many organizations. As a very broad rule of thumb, for example, an organization can tap about 5 percent of the total value of its endowment in any given year to fund operations if they want the endowment to last in perpetuity as noted by the Corporate Finance Institute in their overview of endowment funds. This means that an organization with investments worth $1 million could only tap about $50,000 in revenue in any given year, which even for a small nonprofit is unlikely to cover a meaningful proportion of expenses.

Also worth noting is that just getting to $1 million of funds to invest is very difficult for many nonprofits. According to the National Center for Charitable Statistics, two-thirds of nonprofits in the United States have entire annual budgets of $500,000 or less, meaning for many nonprofits, it would take several years to build that amount, even if adding money to the fund was a priority. Factor in that it is quite common for government and philanthropic funders to explicitly forbid the use of their funds for long-term endowments and building up such a resource is likely not very practical for many nonprofits.

Passive income from something like an endowment comes with several drawbacks, even for organizations that can access it. First, it can create mission-alignment challenges; second, it requires specialty skills; and third, establishing passive income streams can limit flexibility. Mission alignment challenges can take two forms. First, most passive income strategies rely on building up a bolus of assets that generate a smaller revenue stream over time. Doing this often requires a nonprofit to make trade-offs between engaging in more program activities in the present and providing those activities over a longer period. This can be difficult to navigate.

Second, investing whether in securities, real estate, or other asset classes can come with complex ethical concerns and tradeoffs between market efficiency and mission alignment. Should an organization focused on environmental protection invest in fossil fuel companies? What if that investment would generate more revenue for the organization's projects? These complex questions, along with the complexity of the equity markets, where you need to put money to generate this income, means that nonprofits need access to often expensive specialist advice to effectively manage this revenue stream.

Finally, since establishing successful passive revenue streams requires sequestering large amounts of money for long periods of time, pursuing this strategy can restrict an organization's flexibility to respond to change.

As the previous section outlines, earning money to support a nonprofit can be very complicated and requires balancing interrelated benefits and drawbacks across a wide range of revenue streams. As a result, most nonprofits try to hedge by pursuing multiple revenue strategies across all four categories. For example, the Colorado Symphony, based just a few miles from my house, is actively pursuing all four of these revenue streams. According to the Colorado Symphony website, their revenue comes from four primary sources: an allocation of sales tax dollars from a special state fund, sales of tickets to their concerts, interest from their endowment, and charitable contributions.

Each of these categories comes with its own risks, dependencies, and restrictions that need to be managed. Preserving their share of the government funding pool requires maintaining good relationships with local officials and ensuring that the funds stay available, without crossing the line into heavily restricted lobbying activities. The amount of revenue the endowment generates is tied to performance of the capital markets and the quality of the investment management strategy. The symphony must compete with other performing arts organizations and forms of entertainment for wallet share and ticket sales, while also attracting and retaining private donations, many of which are restricted to targeted priorities or require that donors receive specific perks as a *quid pro quo*.

BORROWING MONEY AS A NONPROFIT

For-profit companies and governments can also leverage debt to help smooth out cash flows, raise funds for major infrastructure projects, or fuel expansion of services. In addition to commercial loans or lines of credit, companies can issue shares of common stock or enter private ownership arrangements to access large amounts of funding quickly.

Governments at all levels can issue bonds, and the federal government has even more mechanisms at its disposal for funding. It is true that nonprofits can issue bonds; however, the process is complex, expensive, and only practical for certain types of organizations and projects (Rosenstiel 2016). Only a small percentage of nonprofits, less than 5 percent, are likely to be able to access this type of financing.

This means that most nonprofits face unique constraints on their ability to borrow money, refinance debt, or raise capital. They largely must rely on expensive commercial lending or lines of credit. It forces organizations to be more conservative in how they budget, limits their rates of growth, and contributes to all the deferred maintenance and hand-me-down furniture you see around their offices.

MAKING SENSE OF NONPROFIT FINANCES

Nonprofit finances are complex and have a lot of unique limitations. How can a concerned citizen assess whether a particular organization in their community is financially healthy and well managed? This can be a complicated question, and there are as many methods, ratios, and "rules" as there are experts and ratings websites. Even as someone who works in nonprofits, I find it can be difficult to make sense of how they are calculated, let alone how they apply.

Three of the most common, and most misunderstood or misapplied, are rules about: "overhead," "funding mix," and "sustainability." Many organizations that "rate" nonprofits have, at various points in time, applied versions of these rules when assessing nonprofits. They are also commonly brought into discussions of nonprofit financial health by donors and auditors. Most importantly, these are the rules that have most permeated into the public discussion about charitable giving and nonprofit spending.

OVERHEAD

The principle behind the "overhead" rule is very simple. Nonprofits should align their resources, including money, toward fulfilling their mission and exempt purpose. This basic concept is baked into the legal framework of nonprofits as tax-exempt organizations. For many years, the consensus was that an organization should spend no more than 20 percent of its annual expense budget on "overhead" and dedicate the other 80 percent to "program" expenses. This guidance was used in ratings of nonprofit effectiveness, like the GuideStar seal system, the Charity Navigator star rating system, and others. Many foundations and government agencies also considered it in making funding decisions.

On the surface, it seems like an effective way of translating a basic principle about nonprofits into a simple, consistent rule that can be easily applied to publicly available data. However, under closer scrutiny, the rule doesn't hold up nearly as well. The problem comes from the very simplicity of the premise. It leaves many open questions: Can this rule really be applied to all nonprofits? How do you define overhead? Can those indirect costs have an impact on mission fulfillment?

Ultimately, this rule ends up creating significant problems for the nonprofit sector. First, the ambiguity around the definition of overhead, particularly in the mind of the average citizen, creates an opportunity for bad actors to misrepresent how much they are spending on programs. Seeing nonprofit marketing materials that claim 90 percent or even 98 percent of funds are dedicated to programs is now common. As an experienced nonprofit professional and a person with common sense, this seems more like a gimmick based on some highly creative accounting strategies than a real truth about how any organization operates.

To be clear, I am not suggesting that nonprofits making those claims are engaging in fraud. More accurately, they are being disingenuous. Often, they are stretching the truth on both sides of the balance sheet. On the expense side it is simply stretching reality to claim that certain types of expenses are 100 percent program when that would be difficult to verify. A friend who does bookkeeping for nonprofits has shared stories of organizations where all office supplies are treated as a program cost. I've personally seen organizations where a cocktail reception for fifty donors was treated as a "community program" because two program participants attended.

At bigger organizations, the sleight of hand can get more sophisticated. Several large international NGOs proudly claim that 100 percent of contributions support programming. But if you read the fine print, you discover that it is 100 percent of contributions from certain donors. They just have a separate pool of donors who provide funds to cover their overhead costs.

However, when one group makes a claim like this, it can create pressure for others to match or exceed the claim. This creates the second and more significant problem. Attempting to comply with this rule can adversely impact honest nonprofits, making them less effective by precluding investments in necessary tools to operate efficiently. All in an effort to align with the 80 percent rule and compete with some of the slicker organizations described above.

As a result, it is now the default for nonprofits to defer maintenance, rely on outdated equipment, and keep running software long after the developer stops supporting it. This instinct for thrift in back-office functions becomes a problem when it starts interfering with mission critical work. The hand-me-down furniture at my very first nonprofit job, or at my current job twelve years later, are mostly an aesthetic concern. But the outdated computer software and hardware had practical consequences. It meant that it took longer to serve clients, key records were always at risk of being lost, and it was difficult or impossible to share information to coordinate care.

Amplify this underinvestment in key resources across over a million nonprofits all trying to outcompete one another in the mission alignment hunger games. The consequences of a misunderstood or misapplied "overhead rule" are dire. It doesn't just make the work of nonprofit staff more difficult; it actively makes the whole sector less effective and less innovative.

Fortunately, many of the organizations who championed this rule in the first place have now shifted their perspective, even banding together to create a campaign about "ending the overhead myth." Unfortunately, this concept has been thoroughly embedded in the popular consciousness and aligns quite nicely with some of our deeper cultural ideas about charity work as being "sacrificial" and the virtue of thrift, meaning this well-intentioned but misguided idea persists in the discourse about nonprofit finances.

DIVERSE FUNDING MIX

In general, a diverse funding mix is seen as a stabilizing influence for nonprofits, for many of the reasons outlined in the previous section about nonprofit revenue. The theory goes that by avoiding dependence on any one revenue stream, like a single large donor, event, or source of earned revenue, an organization is at less risk of disruption in its services and operations in response to a sudden change.

To continue the example of the Colorado Symphony, COVID-19 had a significant impact on the symphony's ability to sell tickets for concerts. However, since the organization had consistently invested in building a strong donor base, including corporations and individuals, they were able to keep some revenue coming in the door, allowing them to survive and stay solvent through the uncertainty of 2020. A similar organization that hadn't made those investments might not have survived. The more essential or unique the service might be, the greater the concern about operational continuity and the more important a broad, resilient revenue strategy.

Additionally, managing a diverse funding mix can incentivize organizations to be more attentive and responsive to different groups of stakeholders, as each group is essential to its financial health. In the case of the Colorado Symphony, they certainly want to create concert programs that appeal to classical music fans so they can sell tickets. However, they also need to make sure their offerings appeal to donors and government representatives to stay healthy. In a well-balanced system, the moments of harmony and tension between stakeholders can help to create stronger, more effective organizations and higher quality services.

Intuitively, dedicating resources to cultivating a broad funding mix makes a lot of sense. However, like any generalization in the large, complex nonprofit sector, there are always exceptions and nuances. Obviously, it doesn't make sense to chase diverse revenue streams if the opportunity costs for doing so exceed the potential benefits. However, in a mission-driven organization, like a tax-exempt nonprofit, the opportunity cost, while defined by economic proxies, is often more complex to calculate. Nonprofits exist to fill a wide range of unique and often difficult to measure roles in communities. This can make it difficult to create universal rules for what types of revenue mix are "high risk" or "low risk."

SUSTAINABILITY

Discussion of funding mix might take for granted that it makes sense for an organization to aim for long-term operations, which may not always be the case. This ties into the third big idea, the concept of sustainability. Many philanthropic funders like to home in on sustainability in a way that can feel relentless. As with funding mix and overhead, the concept of sustainability can be broken down into three simple ideas:

1. Most nonprofit missions take years or decades to fulfill. Some may not even have a clear end point.
2. Therefore, nonprofits need to be able to sustain operations over multiple years or even decades to maximize their mission impact.
3. In turn, a funder looking to obtain a particular outcome for a community with their money, should invest in organizations that seem well-positioned to stay operational for years and decades.

The problem is applicability. This very sound reasoning does not apply to every organization and every program. An organization designed to help support a particular event or exhibition, like the 1996 Summer Olympics in Atlanta, doesn't need to be permanent. If the organization is time-limited, it simply may not be possible to establish a well-balanced funding mix, and it doesn't matter if the money runs out.

Similarly, some organizational missions or models require the organization be quite nimble and act with great urgency, like nonprofits formed in response to emergent and acute crises. In those circumstances, it may not make sense to divert staff time and resources away from the urgent work of the organization to invest in building long-term revenue streams and plans. Certainly not right away when the crisis is urgent.

For example, many nonprofits were set up to assist with disaster recovery in New Orleans following Hurricane Katrina. In the immediate aftermath of the storm and the accompanying humanitarian tragedy in the city, restoring essential services to preserve life and health was most essential. Over time, as those needs became less intense, it might have made sense for an organization to focus on sustainability, but it wouldn't have made sense as an immediate priority.

FINANCING "RULES" AND EQUITY IN THE NONPROFIT SECTOR

Not all nonprofits are created equal, nor are the communities they serve. Thus, you cannot have a conversation about nonprofit financing without talking about equity.

The nature of the funding streams themselves, and their potential incompatibility with an organization's mission, can also make building and maintaining a diverse revenue base much more difficult. For example, organizations that serve marginalized groups or provide more stigmatized services might find themselves unable to access major revenue streams, and thus more dependent on smaller, less predictable or efficient sources.

Organizations that focus on providing services to undocumented immigrants can be limited in accepting referrals from government programs and thus may not be able to take advantage of certain types of government contracts. Similarly, organizations like the Harm Reduction Action Center here in Denver, which provides a needle exchange for injecting drug users, are often cut off from public dollars and may struggle to attract other types of donors like corporations. In this case, it makes sense to prioritize the organization fulfilling its purpose, even if that means it is more heavily dependent on fewer revenue streams.

Beyond ensuring that a diverse revenue strategy aligns with an organization's mission, practical and logistical considerations, and the accompanying question of equity can be critically important in understanding the debate on funding mix. Different types of revenue require different levels of investment to operate, and some types of revenue are only available to certain types of organizations. As the saying goes, you have to spend money to make money. This means that those organizations in the position to make larger investments in their revenue streams are more likely to be able to demonstrate that they have sustainable revenue. This is true both in terms of securing charitable donations and earned revenue.

Large scale fundraising events illustrate this point beautifully. The annual fundraiser for The Costume Institute at the Metropolitan Museum of Art in New York, also known as the Met Gala, is one of the most high-profile fundraisers in the world. Setting aside the intangible benefits of hosting such a high-profile event for the museum's brand, the event raised about $13 million in a single night in 2019, according to a report in *Business Insider*. However, the event also costs millions of dollars to produce every year. One estimate, published in *Business Insider*, pegged the cost of hosting the 2016 event at around $3.5 million, which likely excludes the thousands of hours of staff time dedicated to the event each year and the value of in-kind contributions from the likes of Anna Wintour. Events of this type, and all the related financial and intangible benefits, are simply not feasible for the average nonprofit, which likely has an expense budget of under $1 million (Guidestar 2020).

At one job I held, I was tasked with overseeing donor acquisition campaigns with the goal of expanding the organization's donor base to achieve a more balanced funding mix. In the short term, acquisition campaigns can be very expensive, and in my experience, they almost always lose money. In the first few years my organization spent well over $100,000 per year exclusively on acquisition campaigns. The costs helped us to design and produce direct mail and digital ads and "rent" mailing lists to send them to or target and retarget folks online. A single mailing to ten thousand people cost about $25,000 and yielded four new donors and under $400 in revenue. Our results were a bit below the national average, but not unique. According to the Fundraising Effectiveness project, the typical return on a direct mail acquisition campaign is well below 1 percent, meaning even very successful mailings generally lose money in the short term.

Other methods of donor acquisition can be similarly challenging. However, over a longer time horizon, the lifetime value of retaining new donors and the intangible brand awareness benefits associated with using direct mail, digital advertising, and other marketing strategies turns net positive. But much like large scale fundraising events, aggressive donor acquisition campaigns are not accessible to much of the sector. Even for larger organizations, the choice to invest in such a long-term strategy can often be an unattainable luxury.

Nonprofits attempting to earn revenue face similar challenges associated with start-up and operating costs. This is particularly true for nonprofits that sell services in complex markets, like healthcare. Well over 80 percent of healthcare services in the United States are provided by nonprofits. Healthcare billing is complex with specific documentation requirements, specialized accounting practices, and long delays between services rendered and payment tendered. Further, these requirements and practices may vary from payer to payer, with Medicare looking for one thing with a variation required for Medicaid and a private insurer requiring something different.

As a result, both the upfront and operating costs required to earn revenue in the healthcare space from traditional "insurance" payers like Medicare, Medicaid, Blue Cross Blue Shield, and so on are substantial. One study published in the *Journal of the American Medical Association* in 2018 attempted to itemize these costs for academic medical centers. Their analysis found that the staff time and other resources needed to generate and receive payment for a healthcare procedure ranged from about $20 for a primary care check up to $215 for an inpatient surgical procedure (Tseng et al. 2018).

It is worth noting that their analysis was only of academic medical centers, like the Mayo Clinic, and so did not consider the costs of buying and implementing much of the software needed, alongside human staff time. Those software implementation costs can easily run into the hundreds of millions of dollars. For example, the nonprofit University of Vermont Health System announced a plan to spend $151 million on upgrades to its billing infrastructure (Drees 2020). All of these costs are expenses that a nonprofit interested in earning revenue by providing healthcare services would need to be able to front even to have the possible option of making money in that way.

These practical considerations mean that for many nonprofit organizations, particularly those operating with smaller cash reserves and less existing revenue, many sources of income are simply not available to them, leaving them to depend on a smaller number of sources of revenue to survive. This isn't necessarily a reflection of a lack of community buy-in, poor management, or anything else negative. In many cases, it can simply reflect a young or resource-poor organization.

This is where the conversation about equity in the nonprofit sector becomes relevant to this discussion. Nonprofit leader, speaker, and blogger Vu Le captures this issue beautifully and quite succinctly in his blog post on the topic, where he notes that organizations that are more likely to be grassroots and face limitations in what types of revenue streams they can pursue are those led by marginalized and historically disenfranchised groups. These groups rarely have the history of privilege or accumulated capital necessary to stage multi-million dollar galas like historically exclusionary and white-led organizations.

Targeting specific funding streams or sources could be a strategic decision if those sources are better aligned with the mission of the organization. In some cases, it can be counterproductive to pursue new or expanded revenue streams if it would in the short- to medium-term divert funds and other resources away from mission critical work.

Ultimately, the principles behind each of these rules about overhead, sustainability, and funding mix are sound. A nonprofit should always be aligning and optimizing its resources toward fulfilling its mission and purpose. The devil, as always, is in the details. Given the size and complexity of the nonprofit sector, funders need closer analysis and deeper understanding to ensure that these principles are strategically applied to a particular organization.

It might look a bit more like due diligence in the for-profit space. A serious investor considering a significant investment in a particular company is not only going to compare that company to standard guidelines for the sector but is also likely to dig deeper to understand that company's specific market and business model. The investor might also consider their own tolerance for risk and goals before committing their money.

In business, investors who follow their own processes and make creative plays are often rewarded. Whereas nonprofit funders tend to be much more cautious, and sometimes broad principles or rules are misapplied in ways that are counterproductive, reinforcing inequity and slowing progress. In our ever faster moving world, characterized by increasingly complex and large-scale problems, this simply isn't going to cut it.

Also, if a donor or citizen is concerned about the sustainability and health of an organization, I would encourage examination of the composition, practices, and effectiveness of the organization's board just as one does to the organization's liquidity or cash flow from operations. A strong board that has put an effective executive director in place may be able to effectively manage significant financial challenges, whereas an ineffective board may struggle or create the conditions that cause a healthy organization to spiral into crisis.

CHAPTER 3

Trust—It's Complicated

My mind was focused on a weekend of rest and relaxation as I got into the elevator in downtown Denver that smoggy but sunny Friday afternoon in late February. Nailing every detail of the board of directors meeting that had just wrapped up earlier in the week had consumed much of my energy. Now, only one more commitment stood between me and the chance to unplug and unwind for a few days. I was spending the afternoon participating in a volunteer training for graduates of one of our nonprofit's programs who had committed to serve as advocates and spokespeople for the organization. Graduates of this particular program are almost all low-income young women, and many have had to overcome tremendous obstacles like addiction, abuse, or housing and food insecurity during their time in the program.

I made it to the conference room where the group was meeting, helped myself to some snacks from the obligatory veggie tray, and settled in for what I assumed would be a routine training session. I expected a stilted ice breaker and a facilitator reading dutifully from a slide deck to coach the volunteers on their elevator pitches and key facts and figures about the organization.

As I worked toward the end of that week, I felt I was beginning to come into my own in my career. I had been working at this nonprofit for several years and had been promoted twice into a solid middle-management position. Before I knew it, I would be ticking off a decade in nonprofits, and after struggling like Goldilocks with an organization that was too small and informal and then in another that was too big and bureaucratic, I finally felt I found a nonprofit that was "just right" for me.

I always assumed I would work in the public or nonprofit sector, even as a relatively young child. My family was one that paid attention to the news, donated to good causes, and inculcated a focus on the common good.

Thus, when I went off to university, it was with a vision of potential government service or work in a nonprofit fixed firmly in place. My internships and student jobs only fixed this notion more firmly in place as I found on-campus work at the university and my internship with Catholic Charities to be engaging and purposeful. My one semester at a for-profit consulting firm had been a dispiriting exercise in sophistry, inefficiency, and self-importance verging on absurdity.

However, despite my passion and commitment, my transition from student to nonprofit professional hadn't been quick, easy, or glamorous. In those first few years, as I struggled to make ends meet and made the endless round of job interviews, I often envied the seemingly smooth and more financially remunerative careers of my peers in the corporate sector. Fortunately, with persistence, hard work, and a fair amount of good luck, I finally felt like I was finding my stride.

So, despite being ready for a rest, I was generally feeling positive as I arrived in the large conference room where the group was meeting. This afternoon was the group's second training session, and their camaraderie was immediately obvious as they filed into the session laughing and chatting. The session that followed was, refreshingly, not at all what I expected. Instead of passively, politely receiving information, the volunteers really directed the session. Their savvy in discussing how to handle talking with legislators of different parties would have impressed a seasoned lobbyist. "I always play up that I'm a Navy wife with representatives. They love a veteran or a military spouse," shared one volunteer.

Their insights into how to engage and recruit their peers were fresh and creative. When the time came for me to answer questions in the Q&A session, they were incisive and persistent in seeking to understand the strategic direction of the organization. I left work that afternoon invigorated and with a few new ideas to add to my practice in the field. Honestly, I was more inspired by my time with them than during the board meeting filled with corporate luminaries, noted philanthropists, and esteemed academics earlier that week.

The difference was that, unlike in the board meeting, as a mid-level manager I was the most senior staff member that the organization had sent to meet with these volunteers. No one had bothered to review my talking points for this meeting. No senior leaders were overly concerned with the logistics of these meetings or ensuring timely follow up from the CEO.

As I walked back to my apartment that evening, bundled up against the plunging temperatures of dusk in Denver, I reflected on how this afternoon fit into a pattern over my roughly ten years working in various nonprofits. I thought about the time, energy, and attention to detail that are lavished on people with "platforms" and "resources," who served as donors, board members, or thought leaders. While those individuals were genuinely eager to help, and many were incredibly generous with their limited time, expertise, and (perhaps most critically!) money, the advice shared seldom felt actionable or empathetic.

I often left these carefully scripted cups of coffee or choreographed cocktail parties feeling drained or daunted by the new list of to-dos and follow ups. These leaders had indeed been generous in sharing their ideas. This was in marked contrast to the afternoons spent with clients or students whose only "expertise" was often lived experience. Another invaluable resource, I mused, in the times before COVID, when human interaction was still a thing, were those quick check-ins with a colleague at the water cooler or on the park bench in front of the office. These latter conversations, squeezed in around the priority engagements with those seen as experts or rich in resources, were rich in suggestions and often shared efforts that failed, saving each other from "reinventing the wheel."

As I settled in on the sofa in my apartment with a glass of wine and something mindless on Netflix, I continued to think about why the interactions with the donors, government officials, and other influential volunteers and partners were often so draining, while my afternoon spent with those volunteers had felt engaging and rewarding.

It wasn't a matter of intent, as the vast majority of donors and prospective donors I met with were people of good will. They had a genuine desire to affect positive change in their communities and, for the more ambitious, in the wider world. There were certainly difficult or self-interested donors. However, the honest truth was that for every one donor who wanted to know how much it would cost to guarantee their child a slot in the incoming freshman class, or who saw meetings with my colleagues as an elite dating service, there were many more who were sincere, respectful, and committed to making positive impact.

So, what was it that created the space and the drain in those interactions?

The power dynamic certainly mattered, creating an intense scrutiny of every action and comment of a donor and hyper-vigilance about their interests, preferences, and needs. At an organizational level, we needed their time, talent, treasure, and increasingly in our twenty-first century, attention economy, or their platforms, to fulfill our mission. On a personal level, I had metrics to meet, metrics that were tied to my own professional advancement and even continued employment.

Thus, reading the moods and reactions of donors and ensuring their comfort and engagement was of utmost priority in every interaction. Whether it was true or not, in my mind, a joke that didn't land, a cold cup of coffee, or a confusing web form could be the difference between a transformational gift and empty-handed failure. I certainly wasn't the only one who thought that way in engaging with benefactors. I will never forget getting a panicked call from a colleague standing outside her father's funeral. A major donor she had been courting was having difficulty registering for an event. Hundreds of thousands of dollars were at stake, so we leaped into action.

Within five minutes I had comped their ticket, added them to the guest list, and contacted their assistant to apologize profusely for the inconvenience of their own user error in navigating our online registration page. We ended up closing the gift, and while we'll never really know if it hinged on a ticket to that reception, it certainly felt that way to my colleague standing in the snow outside the chapel that morning.

Nonprofits are far from the only organizations where high stakes deals are negotiated or where competition for a limited client base creates strong incentives to go the extra mile. That isn't something that is unique to the sector. Upon reflection, I think the difference is a question of trust and equality in the relationship. The program graduates, who had experienced the organization's services firsthand, were true believers. They had a great deal of trust in the quality of those services and the sincerity of those attempting to deliver them. Further, they saw themselves as genuine peers and partners in the effort to strengthen and grow the organization.

As an externally focused nonprofit staffer, spaces where I was treated with trust and respect were few and far between.

This isn't to say that board members, donors, and others were rude or overtly hostile. Many of them said a lot of the right things, but fundamentally the relationship was rooted in power imbalances and mistrust.

THE TRUST CRISIS IN THE NONPROFIT SECTOR

It turns out my experience and related intuition that many constituents don't particularly trust nonprofits wasn't too far off base. Global trust in nonprofit organizations has steadily decreased over the past several years, according to an extensive study of public trust conducted by global communications firm Edelman. In Edelman's 2021 Trust Barometer report, their analysis found that nonprofits were less trusted than for-profits and that nonprofits had lost ground over the preceding twelve months, by six points in their core trust metric, placing nonprofits as "neutral"—neither trusted nor distrusted.

This metric examines whether citizens see organizations of particular types as competent and ethical. Nonprofits were the only sector to sustain losses in that period. For-profit business, government, and the media all saw gains. Another analysis conducted by Independent Sector, titled the 2021 Independent Sector Trust in Civil Society Survey, had similar findings–it found that trust in nonprofits had remained stable over the past two years but at a fairly low level on their index. These perceptions exist despite there being little actual evidence that nonprofits are any less ethical or competent than other sectors.

Accurate or not, these perceptions have real consequences. Besides making work a draining experience for externally focused nonprofit leaders, this phenomenon also likely plays a role in the stagnant levels of giving to nonprofits over the past forty years, the inefficient models used to fund nonprofits, and the obsession with overhead spending. In short, the mistrust and uneven power dynamics that characterize relationships between the nonprofit sector and its partners in other parts of civil society as well as the government waste time and money depriving communities of needed services and benefits. Thus, it is worth trying to understand what drives it to try to repair it.

A RECIPE FOR TRUST

There are many potential explanations, and it is likely that any number of factors play some role in influencing the degree of trust that people and society collectively have in nonprofits. There is no shortage of experts in both nonprofit practice and academia that have proposed both theories, frameworks, and tactics to explain how trust in nonprofits is generated, is stewarded, and can be increased or decreased. Within this mass of theorizing and analysis, a few common threads that I find resonate with my practical experiences working in nonprofits.

The first is the idea that the relationship between the public and nonprofits is fundamentally different from their relationship with for-profit firms. The College of William & Mary Professor Herrington Bryce identified five distinctive transactions that distinguish firms from nonprofits in his article titled, "The Public's Trust in Nonprofit Organizations: The

Role of Relationship Marketing and Management." Among these are exercising custody over assets for the benefit of society and employing the organization's social capital for public benefit.

Clearly, those are both very different transactions than what most of us would expect from our local CVS or Starbucks. However, in my experience, they are deeply embedded in the conception of what nonprofits are "supposed" to do. For example, one international aid nonprofit that I supported as a volunteer had decided to purchase and operate a farm and hostel as a source of income. This purchase made the nonprofit one of the largest landowners in the community.

Initially, this fact met with positivity. However, when the organization decided to offer standard pay and benefits to local workers and to use conventional farming practices, the response in the community and among donors was swift and negative. To be clear, the practices at the nonprofit were, if anything, slightly more generous and responsible than their for-profit neighbors. But the expectations were much higher that the nonprofit would go above and beyond as stewards of the land and supporters of community members.

The second idea is drawn from economics and is a way of understanding the relationship between nonprofits and the public. The idea is that the relationship between a nonprofit and its community of support is a principal-agent relationship. According to this theory, the public, collectively, is the principal. It delegates certain resources, like donations, to nonprofits as their "agent" to achieve certain desired outcomes.

Principal-agent relationships can absolutely exist in other sectors, and the theory originates with the study of for-profit firms. In the for-profit world, a corporation might hire a law firm to help them successfully purchase intellectual property, like a book from an author. In the space of nonprofits, the outcomes can be much more subjective and intangible. The relationship between the public and a nonprofit's goals are often more ill-defined. For example, the desired outcome of a gift to the symphony might be "supporting classical music as a living art form."

The corollary to this idea is that principals select agents because they have greater expertise or access to information, making them more likely to achieve the desired outcome. However, built into this premise is the idea that information is asymmetrical. This factor makes trust more difficult because part of what the principal may also be looking to gain from the agent is additional information, as well as the outcome.

This is a phenomenon that I, and I would imagine most nonprofit professionals, feel in our bones. Every job I have ever had has featured both a demanding donor who wants every piece of data to make a decision and an interfering board member who is trying to impose their ideas about how to execute processes of which they have no expertise. The ubiquity of this principal-agent dynamic is so great that it can be difficult to isolate specific examples.

Essentially, the public asks more and different things from nonprofits than they do of other types of actors, even the government. They also enter a relationship of special vulnerability with nonprofits, since the outcomes that want nonprofits to achieve are often unique, intangible, and deeply meaningful. Collectively, we entrust nonprofits to embody our better angels. As an outgrowth and blend of deep religious traditions like the Christian virtue of charity, the Jewish concept of *Tikkun olam,* and the best of humanist thinking, the American nonprofit carries unique burdens. The standard structures of marketing and relationships that might work for firms or media outlets are not sufficient to nurture the robust trust that the nonprofit sector needs to thrive.

On a small scale, what I have found does work is a commitment to transparency and authenticity with donors and community members. Part of what built the trust of those volunteers was the long-term, intimate relationships they had with program staff at the nonprofit. As a fundraiser, I have often gotten further by telling a donor the truth or even disagreeing with them than I have in trying to divert or spin them. But the unvarnished, authentic story can be complicated, and expressing it clearly but succinctly is a big task and often feels very risky. It is likely that to achieve a trust reset for the sector at scale will take far more than a few plain-spoken middle managers.

PART 2

CHAPTER 4

High Stakes Philanthropy: The Risks and Rewards of Massive Gifts

―――

One of the most memorable events of my career to date, at least from the perspective of pure pomp and spectacle, was the inauguration of the McCourt School of Public Policy at Georgetown University. Georgetown had long had a public policy institute but lacked the funds to elevate it into a full-blown school with all the associated prestige, level of research activity, and additional revenue. When, after many years of careful negotiation, alumnus Frank McCourt agreed to make the largest gift in university history, $100 million, to launch it, the jubilation in the Office of Advancement, where I had recently come to work, was palpable.

But so was the intensity. We had secured the gift but now had to recognize the most generous donor in the university's history and the launch of a new school in a manner befitting his status. The timeline to accomplish this was just weeks. In that time, we would be hosting at least four major events and many other smaller ones to inaugurate the school. Fetes ranged from a private dinner for the donor to a campus-wide celebration on Healy Lawn. We even had to relocate the gala dinner from the Library of Congress to a tent on the lawn with just days of notice due to a partial government shutdown. The effort: tremendous; the level of precision: military; and the effect: grand, verging on grandiose.

As a new junior staff member, I was assigned to simple tasks that allowed me to stand in the back. I handed out programs and name tags as herald trumpets sounded, choirs sang Latin hymns, and caterers built a chic cocktail bar complete with chaise lounges in a tent on the lawn, all in recognition of Mr. McCourt. The overall spectacle with its choreographed ceremonies, rigid protocol and hierarchy, and religious overtones felt, at least to me, like a royal wedding or state opening of parliament. From my place at the back, it was hard to tell if I was watching a celebration of a collaborative effort to better fulfill Georgetown's mission and live its Jesuit values or a coronation.

To be clear, Georgetown is far from the only organization to embrace pomp and circumstance in celebrating big gifts and ultra-wealthy donors. From the amfAR (American Foundation for AIDS Research) Gala in Cannes to the legendary Met Gala supporting the Costume Institute, the world of philanthropy is full of elaborate celebrations with rigid dress codes, opaque protocols, and exclusive guest lists. All this imitation of aristocratic, old-world tradition is one symptom of a larger trend toward mega-donations from the ultra-rich. This trend creates both opportunity and risk for the nonprofit sector.

Extremely large donations from extremely wealthy families are nothing new. However, they have made a return to prominence in the past fifteen years or so as the United States has entered its second gilded age. Much like the Dukes, Vanderbilts, and Carnegies at the turn of the twentieth century, donors like Frank McCourt are equally eager to confront emergent social challenges while also taking full advantage of opportunities to burnish their images and dabble in a bit of statecraft through their largesse.

Others have written at length about the economic forces that have powered this second gilded age and its sociological and political consequences, as well as the motives of these mega-philanthropists. One book on the subject that is particularly interesting is *Winner Take All: The Elite Charade of Changing the World*, by Anand Giridharadas. Rather than review and restate the arguments Giridharadas and others so eloquently make, this chapter focuses, instead, on how their giving is shaping (or distorting) the behavior of the nonprofit sector in ways that ultimately undermine trust and weaken the sector's effectiveness in fulfilling its larger societal purpose.

In terms of their impact on nonprofits, megadonors' influence isn't only about the size of their gifts. Megadonors' giving can convey prestige, help to secure other forms of support, and is often essential for an organization to fulfill its mission. As outlined in the chapter on nonprofit structure and finances, many nonprofits need private philanthropic support to stay afloat. Whether the donations provide capital for new buildings, enhanced or expanded services, or simply fund daily operations, organizations depend on those dollars.

We also know that around 80 percent of philanthropic dollars across the sector come from individuals, including individually directed giving vehicles like donor-advised funds or bequests, something that has been consistently true for at least the past fifteen years (Hadero 2021). Thus, the behavior and trends of this group of donors is crucially important to the overall financial health of the nonprofit sector.

Within this essential revenue stream, nonprofits are increasingly dependent on a smaller number of individuals making larger gifts. Although the total dollars given to nonprofits has continued to grow alongside the larger economy, the share of Americans who donate to nonprofits has shrunk steadily over time, declining from about 66 percent of adults in 2000 to only 53 percent in 2016, according to a report from the University of Indiana and Vanguard Charitable. The same report found that, logically, the average gift size has grown as well, increasing from about $1,180 in the year 2000 to about $1,400 in 2016. Finally, the analysis also found that demographics of giving have also followed predictable trends with older, wealthier individuals being most likely to donate and to donate a higher percentage of their income or wealth.

Over this same period, the number of nonprofits eligible to receive from those funds has grown by about 10 percent (Urban Institute 2022). This means that there is greater competition for the time, attention, and treasure of this shrinking pool of donors. This manifests in an increasingly sophisticated "arms race" to attract and retain individual donors, one example of which is the increasingly elaborate donor recognition celebrations popping up all over the world.

This challenge also creates stronger incentive to maximize the value of the donors nonprofits do acquire, since the process of acquiring them is increasingly slow and expensive due to that increased competition. According to the Association of Fundraising Professionals, in general, it costs about $1.25 to raise $1 from a new donor, meaning that to achieve a net positive return you need the donor to make multiple gifts, as renewal gifts generally have about an 80 percent rate of return (Axelrad 2022).

Basically, it costs about $31 to raise a new $25 donation. But, renewing an existing donor for a gift of the same amount costs about $5. So, if I can persuade the donor to give twice, I spend about $36 and raise about $50, netting me $14. If I can persuade the donor to increase their gift amount on the second gift, the math gets even better.

However, this retention piece is increasingly difficult, too, as the average donor retention rate has also steadily dropped. According to an analysis conducted by the Association of Fundraising Professionals as part of the Fundraising Effectiveness Project, in 2020 only 19.2 percent of first-time donors made a second gift within twelve months. The same report found that between 2019 and 2020 the overall donor retention rate across nonprofits dropped as well, falling to 43.6 percent, meaning that less than half of donors who gave to a particular nonprofit in 2019 made another gift to that same nonprofit in 2020.

This challenging backdrop creates important context to understand the powerful attraction that mega-donors have for nonprofits and the increasingly essential role that the whims of ultra-high net worth individuals can play in picking winners and losers in the sector. For organizations facing fierce competition to achieve even modest growth in their philanthropic revenue, a multimillion-dollar check from Mackenzie Scott is nothing short of a *Deus ex machina* moment. Similarly, for nonprofits in capital-intensive parts of the sector, like higher education or art museums, these massive gifts are nothing short of essential to achieving their goals.

And ultimately, what is wrong with the very wealthy making gifts proportional to their resources? If you set aside the very real ethical concerns about the sources of the gifts, the money undoubtedly does a lot of good for the organizations that receive it. These transformational gifts can make it to nonprofits much faster or with greater flexibility than other types of income.

This drives the problem because it makes even the possibility of receiving a principal or transformational gift so alluring that even the most disciplined nonprofit leader can lose sight of the potential risks. Although they are less visible, there can absolutely be major risks from depending upon or even just accepting these seven-, eight-, and even nine-figure gifts. In general, these negative impacts fit into four closely related categories:

1. mission creep
2. conflicts of interest

3. power imbalances
4. perpetuating inequity

MISSION CREEP

The first risk is the mission creep that even the act of chasing big gifts can create. In an effort to catch the eye of big donors, nonprofits might be tempted to stray from their core missions or embrace ideas and approaches that are foreign or even conflict with the needs and values of other stakeholders.

A very well-documented case study of this phenomenon comes from the Bill & Melinda Gates Foundation. In the 2010s the Bill & Melinda Gates Foundation launched an ambitious project related to K–12 education in the United States, called Intensive Partnerships for Effective Teaching. The program made significant direct investments of about $290 million collectively in five school systems, including a nonprofit coalition of Charter School Management Organizations.

According to a press release from the Bill & Melinda Gates Foundation, the nonprofit received about $60 million in grant funding. The funds were to be used to implement sweeping changes in how teachers were selected, evaluated, and offered professional development with the goal of improving student outcomes. Given the dramatic changes to established personnel policies and systems, it is not surprising that the implementation created significant "political turmoil" for the nonprofit, as noted by Jay Greene, a professor at the University of Arkansas, in a blog post for *Education Next*.

Unfortunately, the Intensive Partnership program failed to deliver on its many ambitious goals, with no significant progress made on most indicators that the foundation had identified for the project. In some cases, there was even backsliding, as outlined in a detailed evaluation of the initiative led by the RAND corporation.

To be clear, there is no reason to believe that anyone either on the nonprofit side or at the foundation went into the partnership with anything but good intentions, quality experts, and thorough research. However, in accepting this large and prestigious gift, the nonprofit assumed greater risk than the foundation. It put its mission fulfillment, trust with the educator community, and ultimately long-term sustainability on the line.

The foundation can comparatively easily "fail forward" and continue to work and invest in K–12 education with minimal, if any, damage to its reputation. Why? Because the foundation can shift responsibility for this failure to other partners more easily. They are just offering resources, and if there were issues with the execution of the plan, clearly that is the responsibility of the grantee. However, following this failure, the nonprofit now faces the work of rebuilding trust and relationships, reestablishing credibility, and securing new funds.

Although we can never be certain, it isn't hard to imagine that the temptation of large payments, and the prestige and financial security that come with them, could encourage leaders, including board members, to minimize the gravity of the risks or discount the probability of a negative outcome. It might also make them willing to embrace approaches or techniques not clearly aligned with the organization's values. This leads to the second challenge: conflict of interest.

CONFLICT OF INTEREST

The second issue, conflict of interest, is closely related to mission creep. The potential individual benefits for nonprofit leaders who secure big gifts can create misaligned incentives between the organization and its leadership. For many nonprofit leaders and board members, the prestige and access associated with securing mega-gifts is a reward in itself. Successfully securing such gifts can be essential to professional advancement, securing bonuses, or even just retaining one's position.

The bonuses on the table can be substantial. One analysis conducted by Inside Higher Ed of more than one hundred public university presidents' contracts found that bonuses associated with performance ranged from 10 percent to 20 percent of base salary, or between $13,000 and $200,000 dollars with an average of around $80,000. The study also found that among those contracts that specified performance metrics, all had fundraising and revenue targets to earn maximum bonuses. In my own professional experience, I am frequently asked about the largest gift I've ever raised or who is on my list of prestigious connections when I interview for fundraising or executive director roles.

Clearly, these are meaningful considerations about personal success and advancement for nonprofit leaders and fundraisers. They can be substantial enough to create a conflict of interest when nonprofit leaders consider which projects to take on or gifts to accept. The possibility of a big bonus or promotion could induce them to embrace a project that isn't a good fit for the organization's values or has major long-term risks. Wise organizations often try to prevent this through gift acceptance policies requiring more than just one leader to sign off on major projects. However, if all the people involved in the process have similar incentives, it isn't a very effective tool.

POWER IMBALANCE

The third issue is the imbalance that big gifts can create for the finances and, therefore, the distribution of power within nonprofits. As discussed in the chapter on how nonprofits are financed, the general "best practice" is to seek diversified, blended revenue streams. This is not only prudent from the perspective of insulating the organization from financial shocks, but also to keep any one individual or group from having excessive influence over the organization.

However, because of their sheer size, the seven-, eight-, or nine-figure gifts from ultra-wealthy donors are often difficult, if not impossible, to balance or replace. This can give that single donor disproportionate influence over organizational decision-making. Over the course of my career, I have come across donors that stipulate the right to choose board members, approve changes to the organizational management team, or even approve organizational branding.

Essentially, the organization's financial dependence can, in turn, hollow out the influence of other important stakeholder groups, like program beneficiaries, smaller donors, or policymakers. If these groups feel ignored, they may become disengaged or even abandon the organization. This, in turn, is likely to make the organization that much more dependent on that single donor. This creates a negative feedback loop that reduces trust in the organization and, ultimately, weakens its ability to fulfill its mission.

PERPETUATING INEQUITY

The fourth issue is the systemic inequity in the opportunity to even ask for a seven-figure or larger gift. Many nonprofits, particularly newer organizations, those serving exclusively low-income communities, and those led by people of color, do not even have the opportunity to be considered for these kinds of gifts.

First, ultra-wealthy donors rarely make themselves easily accessible to nonprofits seeking gifts. The same is true of their foundations and other giving vehicles. The Bill & Melinda Gates Foundation, from my earlier example, doesn't accept unsolicited letters of inquiry or proposals. It is the same at the Chan Zuckerberg Initiative and countless other high-profile foundations, corporate giving programs, or community foundations.

From the perspective of individual philanthropists, this is mostly a function of volume. There are well over 1.5 million nonprofits in the US, and only about 110,000 ultra-high net worth individuals, so responding to all that outreach could become quite overwhelming (Statista 2021). However, it can also be a function of financial incentives associated with being in the orbit of the ultrawealthy. When there is a lot of money on the table, there are a lot of people hoping for a cut of the action. It is certainly in the best interest of a money manager looking for job security to gatekeep access to philanthropists, the goal being more to prop up their own value proposition and fee structure, rather than because the response is truly overwhelming, or the issues are truly that complex.

As a result, contact with ultra-wealthy individuals generally must be made indirectly. Much to the chagrin of grassroot nonprofit board members who are forever suggesting that the executive director just email Jeff Bezos or Michael Bloomberg. Securing a contact with someone like that generally requires working through money management intermediaries or through cultural intermediaries like think tanks or universities. Alumni weekends, think tank fellowships, and trendy "convenings" like the Aspen Ideas Festival are all powerful tools to take the first step toward a multi-million-dollar gift.

However, even getting access to the intermediaries often takes either a well-placed connection to make introductions or detailed research and a bit of good luck. Relationships must also be carefully cultivated and maintained. All of this takes time, skill, and money, meaning it helps to be a nonprofit that already has some resources at its disposal. It also helps to be a nonprofit that provides services that are used by wealthy people, like elite universities, cultural institutions, or research hospitals.

As a result, the organizations that get most of these massive contributions are generally already large and well established, in the sub-parts of the sector outlined above. In fact, according to the 22nd Annual Philanthropy 50, a roundup of the biggest gifts made in 2021, 86 percent of the tens of billions of dollars in giving counted in the round up went to either healthcare systems, schools and universities, or into donor-advised funds (Di Mento 2022).

In turn, these organizations are more likely to be white-led and male-led than smaller, less-established organizations. So, whether intentionally or not, the way that massive gifts are distributed in the sector reinforces underinvestment in leaders of color and communities of color.

Also worth noting is that, in addition to perpetuating injustice, the process by which most mega-donors give is likely to have a negative impact on innovation in the sector since it is so difficult for newer, smaller players to access these kinds of investments. No matter how much better the approach, if it competes against an organization with millions of dollars in the bank, it is likely to struggle. The few that do succeed tend to share some of the same characteristics above, particularly access to the cultural intermediaries.

On this last point, in the past year or two there has been some movement to try to rectify this problem of access to these types of opportunities. However, the system itself is flawed and characterized by unacceptable power imbalances. These imbalances require a more sweeping solution than just opening the "back channels" for accessing, sometimes distorting, or destabilizing mega-gifts to more traditionally marginalized groups. Ultimately, the problem isn't who gets past cultural or financial gatekeepers. It is the fact that there is such an arbitrary, conflict-vulnerable apparatus surrounding some of the most generous philanthropic giving.

If the ultrawealthy are committed to maximizing their impact, not just on pet projects but for the nonprofit sector, they would be wise to consider how they can evolve their approach. Failure to do so is likely to further erode trust in the nonprofit sector, yield a continued decline in the number of smaller donors, and sustain ongoing inequity.

CHAPTER 5

Inclusion and Incentives: The Power of Nonprofit Boards

Since most nonprofits follow a corporate structure, they almost all have boards of directors or trustees. Just like for-profit corporations, boards vest great power to influence the impact and effectiveness of an organization in a small group of people. However, unlike many for-profit companies, nonprofits are much more likely to be the primary or even sole providers of essential community services. This means the stakes for the select group of individuals that comprise nonprofit boards and the communities they serve are very high.

Nonprofit boards need to work. Unfortunately, all too often they don't, and the consequences are real. To understand why this matters and how to improve on it, it is useful to know what boards do, who serves on them, and how they interact with other parts of the community.

WHAT DO NONPROFIT BOARDS DO?

Anyone who has ever worked, or even interned, in a nonprofit has experienced the sudden adrenaline and activity associated with a board meeting. The best conference room gets spruced up, and budget dollars suddenly appear for mineral water and the specific brand of diet ginger ale that the board chair likes. Staff members pull late nights to polish and proofread detailed reports, spreadsheets, and slide decks. Everyone is focused on creating a seamless experience and putting their best foot forward for the small group of directors—a group empowered to make the biggest decisions for the organization. These directors are also often among its largest financial supporters. In large organizations, like the university where I once worked, there are often entire teams of staff who focus on board operations to choreograph the careful dance of the organization's executives and the board.

Why does a board meeting provoke such a strong response from the staff? In part, it is because of the board's role as one of the few legally required structures for most nonprofits. Most nonprofits in the United States are organized as corporations, under relevant state laws and regulations. As corporations, nonprofits are required to have boards of directors. The board at a nonprofit is ultimately responsible for the governance of the organization, including acting as fiduciary (Foundation Group 2022).

These governance responsibilities are often summed up as the duties of care, loyalty, and obedience. The duty of care requires that a director act as a reasonably prudent person would in carrying out the activities of the organization. The duty of loyalty requires that directors place the organization's interests ahead of their own in making decisions, including disclosing potential conflicts of interest. Finally, the duty of obedience requires that directors ensure the organization operates in compliance with relevant laws and regulations and in alignment with its stated exempt purpose (Long 2018). As is the case with for-profit corporations, directors can be held personally liable for the actions of the organization. In many states, that can even extend to criminal prosecution (Long 2018). So, for most nonprofits, the buck really does stop with the board on many critical issues.

Beyond that basic legal framework, nonprofit boards have wide discretion in how they operate. As a result, the day-to-day role of the board can vary significantly between nonprofits. These differences are driven by a number of factors, including the organization's budget, number of staff, level of maturity, and board member preferences. Most commonly, boards in smaller organizations with less budget and fewer professional staff will play a bigger role in operations, with board members volunteering to do bookkeeping, write newsletters, or plan events. In larger organizations, it is more unusual for board members to be involved in routine activities and management decisions (National Council of Nonprofits 2022).

Regardless of size, boards fulfill certain responsibilities on behalf of the organization. These include financial management and oversight tasks, such as reviewing the organization's IRS Form 990 (a required tax filing), commissioning and reviewing an independent audit of the organization's financial records, and approving the annual budget. The board also hires and provides performance management to the executive director or chief executive of the organization and partners with that person in developing the organization's strategic plan. Finally, in most cases the board is responsible for its own operations, including its bylaws, policies, and membership (BoardSource 2016).

There are several organizations, both nonprofit and for-profit, that provide guidance on best practices, and some donors or other funders might establish certain requirements for governance practices as a condition of receiving financial support. However, by and large, boards are permitted to self-police within the comparatively loose framework of state laws governing corporations.

Collectively, these responsibilities for setting strategy, ensuring financial stability, and selecting the organization's operational leader give the board members of nonprofit organizations significant influence over the success or failure of the organization they govern. The flexibility and latitude that boards are given to self-police can result in bad outcomes for the organization and the community they are intended to serve, particularly if the result is a board that is an insiders group, outsources responsibilities for hiring and oversight under the guise of "consulting," or is ethically compromised in some way.

One very common, but critical, way that the latitude boards are given can create a poor outcome is through self-selection. Most nonprofit boards are allowed to self-select members, with very limited outside scrutiny, and most boards are quite small. According to an analysis by the industry group BoardSource, the median nonprofit board has thirteen members.

Since board seats are relatively exclusive, and new board members are selected by the existing membership, there is a strong potential for cronyism to creep into the board selection process. This creates a strong incentive for prospective board members to prioritize schmoozing current board members to secure a nomination or seat on the board. This creates a system where the social capital associated with being at the "right" schools or in the "right" job for networking, or deep pockets to make generous donations are essential to gain a board seat. In some cases, those criteria may even trump professional skills or relevant lived experiences.

WHO SERVES ON BOARDS?

The result is that membership on nonprofit boards favors older white people and often fails to reflect the communities they serve. On that latter point, in the Leading with Intent (LWI) Survey, the largest national survey of nonprofit boards, only about a third of the nonprofit leaders questioned felt that their boards reflected the demographics of the community that they served. The LWI Survey also found that despite some improvements, white people over forty continue to be overrepresented on boards compared to the general population. In fact, Fast Company reported that the percentage of all-white boards in the nonprofit sector increased from 25 percent to 27 percent between 2015 and 2017 (Paynter 2017). For example, only 5 percent of board members identified as Latinx, even though Latinx people make up about 18 percent of the population, according to the US Census Bureau.

Board members skew older than the general population, as noted in "The Impact of Diversity: Understanding How

Nonprofit Board Diversity Affects Philanthropy, Leadership, and Board Engagement." This study found that people over forty comprised about 83 percent of board members as compared to 61 percent of the general population.

The team working on that study also found that disparities in gender, ethnicity, and age were more pronounced in older organizations and those with larger budgets, where older men are more dominant, and these disparities do not seem to be improving over time (Lilly School of Philanthropy 2018).

Although representation for LGBTQIA+ individuals in board roles is roughly proportional to the norm, a study of nonprofit private foundations found that of the foundation staff members and board members who responded that they were LGBT+, more than half were closeted in the workplace. Alarmingly, the numbers were higher for those in board roles than those in staff roles (Funders for LGBTQ Issues 2018).

Some of these disparities, for example the tendency of boards to skew older as they often target people with significant professional experience and stature for members, are unsurprising. However, the overall picture that this data paints is a concerning one. The lack of diversity and misalignment between the communities that many nonprofits serve, and their most senior leaders pose several problems related to organizational effectiveness and citizen trust in nonprofits. This is especially true at "safety net" nonprofits providing essential services in low-income communities. The gravity of these problems is amplified by the pattern that larger organizations, who may provide services to more people or have greater community influence, tend to have the older, whiter, more male boards.

Research conducted by multiple organizations, including BoardSource, the Lilly Family School of Philanthropy at Indiana University, and others, indicates that boards that are less diverse are also less effective in fulfilling their roles, particularly around advocacy, fundraising, and organizational leadership. As noted in "The Impact of Diversity," although the relationship between board demographics and board effectiveness is complex, in general, boards where the proportion of women and people under thirty-nine was higher performed better across almost every measure of key board activities, including governance.

In my own experience, a key determinant of board effectiveness is also relevant, lived, and practical experience. A start-up nonprofit that I advised was interested in providing healthcare services to people experiencing homelessness. The organization's board was very passionate but was exclusively composed of well-off folks who had little or no firsthand experience with people in this population. As a result, they didn't know much about the various public programs, like Medicaid, that many unhoused people participate in or the technology used to access them. They also all spoke fluent English and had the benefit of advanced degrees. They had big blind spots around things like translation services, access to smartphones, or how payments from Medicaid were made to nonprofits. This made it very difficult for them to make effective decisions about a funding model or ask the right questions about the organizational budget.

Boards that don't reflect the community can also contribute to reduced public trust in the competence and ethics of the nonprofit sector, particularly among groups that have traditionally been marginalized or underserved, like BIPOC communities.

Regardless of whether the public perception is accurate or not, it can have consequences for fundraising, service utilization, and even hiring of staff. Conversely, if a board, as the representatives of an organization, has strong personal ties in the community, that can be a significant boost to trust in the organization, as noted in "The Independent Sector's Trust in Civil Society Report."

On a personal level, in my own career, I am often wary of applying for jobs at organizations where the board appears to be composed solely of older, white men. When considering these roles, I must wonder whether the organization will be welcoming and inclusive of me as a gay, younger professional and member of the LGBT+ community. Anecdotally, I know many of my colleagues, who are people of color or women, harbor similar concerns and might choose not to apply for or accept a position at a nonprofit where the senior-most leadership doesn't reflect society as a whole or the population that the group is attempting to serve.

I am not alone in these concerns. A broad survey of over 1,600 nonprofit professionals conducted by the Level Playing Field Institute and Common Good Careers affirmed this intuition. In this survey, 17 percent of all respondents, and 35 percent of respondents of color, noted that they had withdrawn from a search or declined a job offer due to a perceived lack of diversity in an organization's culture and leadership (Schwartz et al. 2016). Thus, organizations with boards that lack diversity may be losing out on top talent to staff their organizations.

While individually each of these data points can seem esoteric, the impact on organizations and their constituents can be very real. Board composition can make or break the effectiveness of the organization and can play a critical role setting the tone for a positive, trusting relationship with its constituents. Even though boards that mirror society by including people from diverse backgrounds, genders, races, and ages are more effective and more trusted, nonprofit boards are still disproportionately older, whiter, and wealthier.

In addition to homogenous membership, many boards lack the knowledge, experience, or will to operate efficiently and effectively. As with selecting their membership, nonprofit boards have broad latitude in setting and enforcing policies around board member conduct, organizational oversight, and financial controls. In theory, as a part of their duty of care, nonprofit board members are held to the standard of reasonable judgment in making decisions about the organization and are encouraged to seek guidance from experts like lawyers or accountants in acting on behalf of the organization.

Beyond this broad guidance, there is a lot of room for ineffective board leadership. Disengaged or dysfunctional boards can have major impacts not only on organizations but also the clients they serve. Since nonprofits are often key safety net organizations, this can be a significant problem for the community. Additionally, regardless of board composition, ineffective leadership also undermines trust in the nonprofit sector, reduces access to services, and can ultimately exacerbate the societal problems the organization is attempting to solve.

As with board recruitment, when left to self-police, boards often fail. The same Leading with Intent survey that identified the representation issues with nonprofit boards found that less than a third of nonprofits had implemented industry standard practices around financial oversight (Boardsource 2021). In addition, only about a quarter of those responding to the survey had clear operational continuity policies in place in case of the unexpected departure or incapacitation of the executive director or other key leaders. Clearly, this is a problem, and one that could have significant implications for a nonprofit's well-being.

Since the board is entrusted with making organizational decisions with great consequence, the risks associated with failure are very high, threatening the very existence of the organization. This, in turn, can be devastating to a community that is depending on that nonprofit.

WHO CAN PROVIDE OVERSIGHT?

One extreme example of how neglect or even malfeasance by a nonprofit board can have disastrous consequences is the Florida Coalition Against Domestic Violence (FCADV). This organization was established to serve as an intermediary in helping to distribute state funds and provide technical assistance to local domestic violence services organizations, essentially administering all the state's domestic violence support services. As such, it was the only organization in the state of Florida playing this role. As a nonprofit, it had significant contracts with the state in addition to raising funds from a variety of private donors.

In 2020, its CEO and board of directors became embroiled in a high-profile set of lawsuits, investigations, and hearings in the state legislature related to the compensation of its long-serving CEO, Tiffany Carr. The state alleges that Carr was paid excessive compensation up to $7.5 million dollars over a period of several years. Additionally, allegations surfaced in the press of substandard services provided to the organization's grantees and partners (Reeves 2020).

As with most nonprofits, the board of directors was responsible for setting Carr's compensation and approving the terms of her employment. Over the course of the investigation and legal discovery process, it became clear that there were potential conflicts of interest between the board members and the CEO, as several board members were also leaders at organizations that received sub-grants or contracts from FCADV. In some cases, these awards amounted to as much as 50 percent of their organizational budgets (Haughey 2020). If this is true, it would suggest that the board members may have violated their duty of loyalty to FCADV by putting the interest of their personal organizations ahead of FCADV's.

In testimony before the Florida State House of Representatives' Integrity and Ethics committee, three board members seemed to suggest that they hadn't fully reviewed the terms of Carr's employment contract and were unfamiliar with the basic terms they had approved, a clear violation of the duty of care.

While the interlocking lawsuits, countersuits, and investigations continued to unravel in spring of 2020, FCADV was placed in receivership, and ultimately the responsibilities of the organization were placed under the direct control of the Florida Department of Children and Families. However, all the transitions created significant disruptions and delays in the provision of critical domestic violence services at the height of the COVID-19 pandemic. Knowing the exact impact is difficult, but it is quite possible that the failure of the board at FCADV to properly discharge its responsibilities is the root cause of the deaths of Floridian victims of domestic violence as noted by a state legislator during the hearing (Haughey 2020).

This story highlights not only how nonprofit boards can fail to perform their core functions for years at a time but also the very real consequences of those failures often for the most vulnerable in a community.

What's worth noting is that a significant part of why this issue of executive compensation and related issues of poor services provided to vulnerable Floridians is even coming to the attention of the public is that the organization had contracts with the state that allowed more extensive oversight and engagement.

If the organization were exclusively privately funded, it would have been up to an individual donor or other stakeholder to raise the issue of the board members' probity, either by filing a complaint or suing the organization—both of which would require extensive knowledge, resources, and commitment. Also worth noting is that part of why this issue has proven to be so complex is because of the flexibility and broad room for interpretation that exists in much of the guidance around nonprofit boards and nonprofits generally.

In most states, the nonprofit regulatory system is structured with plenty of vague terms like "excessive" or "unreasonable," designed to give boards flexibility and discretion in leading organizations. It leaves the determination of what meets those vague standards to the courts. The problem is that when issues come up, the avenue for resolution is slow, expensive litigation. Litigation that only a very small number of well-resourced and highly committed individuals could support for any given organization. The result of this system is that there is frequently little practical accountability for boards operating in ineffective, unethical, or even illegal ways.

In most cases, the consequences are not nearly as dire as those in the case of FCADV. However, even when the impact is simply a lost grant or strategic misstep, the consequences for the community can be meaningful, and a major scandal like the FCADV fiasco can do irreparable damage to public trust not just for that organization but in the sector as a whole.

HOW MIGHT WE COLLECTIVELY MAKE BOARDS WORK BETTER?

The flexibility of boards and the nonprofit corporate structure is something that helps nonprofits to be nimbler and more innovative in responding to community needs. At their best, boards can provide invaluable expertise, bridge critical linkages to the community, and ensure the financial health and stability of the organizations they steward. In practice, it is all too common for nonprofit boards to provide ineffective and even unethical oversight to organizations that they are entrusted to guide as fiduciaries. Further, because of their selection processes, they can serve to reinforce unjust and exclusionary structures in society. Particularly alarming is that, at least according to available evidence, this is as common in large, well-established organizations playing vital roles in the community as in fragile start-up organizations.

How can those both inside and outside the nonprofit sector respond constructively to these challenges?

First, the *laissez-faire* approach to nonprofit boards is not serving the nonprofit sector or society to maximum benefit. While such an approach might be acceptable in the sink-or-swim for-profit marketplace, for nonprofits that serve as essential safety nets or custodians of irreplaceable cultural artifacts, greater accountability is needed.

There is a clear role for policymakers in reorienting the approach to nonprofit boards away from using the courts to clean up messes when things go wrong and toward placing appropriate guardrails and support in place to encourage nonprofits to act effectively and in service to the community.

Immediate areas of focus could include greater transparency in board selection, improving pathways for accessible dispute resolution, and more proactive training requirements for board members. Further ideas and how states might move in this direction are included in the chapter on public policy.

I would also encourage donors to prioritize investing in organizations with diverse boards that represent the communities the nonprofits serve and society at large. Seek opportunities to support boards, through donations, engagement, employment, and funding, that implement policies and practices including transparency and accountability. Donors can also intentionally create space, through their financial donations, for nonprofits to enhance board members and staff to access training and other resources to support efficient, ethical operations.

Additionally, all active citizens should learn more about the boards at nonprofits in their communities to understand who serves on them and what role they play. They should also consider volunteering to serve on a board themselves to bring their experience and commitment into the sector. The final piece in this puzzle would be creating tools or structures for nonprofits across the sector to share best practices and create authentic mutual accountability.

CHAPTER 6

Nonprofits and Government: Moving from Passive to Partner

Nonprofit organizations are a critical, distinctive part of the social fabric of the United States. As they work to fulfill their missions, they also play other essential roles. They form an integral part of the social safety net as the backbone of our entire healthcare infrastructure. Further, they play a significant role in education and child development, steward critical cultural resources, conserve the environment, and meet dozens of other needs, priorities, and passions for citizens. Roles that have only become more critical with the rise of the hollow state and increased contracting out of government programs and services to the nonprofit sector (Milward 1994).

Additionally, nonprofits employ tens of millions of Americans (Salamon 2019). Further, charitable contributions alone make up about 2 percent of our national gross domestic product each year, amounting to hundreds of billions of dollars

(Giving USA 2020). When the entire picture is considered, the economic impact of the nonprofit sector is likely in the trillions of dollars annually.

Furthermore, with comparatively low barriers to entry and broad flexibility in structure and form, the classic 501(c)(3) nonprofit also drives innovation and permits flexibility and agility in responding to community needs and citizen passions.

The vibrancy and scale of the nonprofit sector can also come with a dark side. The sector is not immune nor exempt from participating in racism, misogyny, and elitism. In fact, the nonprofit sector can play a corrosive role in the social fabric by concentrating social capital and decision-making authority in the hands of a small number of wealthy individuals, undermining the democratic process and stifling critical voices. In addition, the flexibility and ease of access to the sector can divert resources and focus away from evidence-based or community-driven solutions.

These risks highlight some of the reasons that public policymakers at all levels of government should be highly attentive to the nonprofit sector. A changing nonprofit landscape, with more mega-donors and the potential for consolidation of influence, make oversight of this sector imperative. Currently, it is often the case that when overseeing the nonprofit sector, government officials are primarily reactionary. They swoop in to address a scandal or happily pose for pictures at the opening of a new community center but pay little attention to the day-to-day.

As noted in the chapter on the history of nonprofits, comparatively little has changed in the basic structure and framework that creates exempt organizations in the past thirty years, at either the federal or state levels. That is not to say there haven't been any shifts. In general, three trends have dominated policy making at the state and federal levels:

1. **Increased delegation of administration** and associated oversight of government programs and services as well as program and service delivery to the nonprofit sector. The trend of contracting out has continued to increase. This increase has resulted in the burdens of government falling more frequently to nonprofits.
2. **Changes in the structure and incentives for charitable giving.** This has primarily happened at the federal level through the expansion of donor-advised funds facilitated by the Pension Protection Act of 2006 (Public Law 2006, 109–280). The increase in the standard deduction that was part of the Tax Cuts and Jobs Act of 2017 and consequent reduction in the number of Americans itemizing their deductions has also disrupted incentives for donors to give, particularly donors making more modest contributions (Public Law 2017, 115–97).
3. **Increased demands for data and transparency.** Particularly at the state level, regulators have increased requirements for more nonprofits to provide more data to register as nonprofits in their respective states. This comes on top of the longstanding federal informational return filing requirement, the IRS 990 Form.

Unfortunately, these changes are not generally supportive of the nonprofit sector in achieving its central goals. In many cases these policy trends disincentivize innovation and disadvantage smaller and start-up nonprofits, including those founded and based in underserved or historically disenfranchised communities.

On the surface, requests for transparency and increased reporting requirements for nonprofits at the state level are a sensible strategy. By requiring more disclosure, states can reduce nonprofit fraud and demonstrate nonprofit efficiency. In practice, however, this approach just disadvantages smaller nonprofits and those with fewer resources, since in many cases they are more burdened by reporting on all these metrics and have less expertise to navigate requirements.

Similarly, the expansion of donor-advised funds and the increase in the standard deduction on income taxes have combined to reshape the philanthropic giving landscape to be more competitive by creating incentives for fewer donors to make larger gifts less frequently. As discussed previously, the proportion of citizens who make gifts to nonprofits has steadily dropped. The average gift size has also gone up. In this more competitive environment, it is more difficult for startup nonprofits to gain traction, especially those that are not closely tied to well-resourced communities in the first place.

The expansion of Donor-Advised Funds (DAFs), enabled as part of larger legislation during the Bush administration, is incredibly counterproductive (Public Law 2006, 109–280). In short, a DAF is a mechanism by which an individual can get a tax deduction simply by committing to give that money to some 501(c)(3) at some future date (Curtis 2022). In the meanwhile, the money can sit in a bank or investment account indefinitely. Unlike private foundations, donor-advised funds have no minimum annual payout. Although the concept of the DAF has been around since the 1930s, the 2006 legislation created a clearer path for them to be widely implemented (Curtis 2022). The end result is that money that in prior years might have flowed directly into nonprofits is now sitting in DAFs, which are often managed at a profit by private sector investment firms like Fidelity or Charles Schwab.

In my own work as a fundraiser, I have seen the proportion of donors giving through DAFs skyrocket. Alongside that, I have often seen donors reduce the frequency and overall amount of their giving. One donor I had worked with for many years stopped giving entirely for several years as they were focused on building up the funds in the DAF to make a bigger gift. Although that is the exception, donors who used to give monthly or twice a year now make one annual gift. That gift might be larger, but it usually doesn't match their previous tradition of multiple gifts in amount. This all has made revenue streams even more unpredictable for nonprofits.

The amount sitting in these DAFs is significant. "The 2021 DAF Report" published by the National Philanthropic Trust estimated that in 2020 alone, individuals contributed over $47 billion to DAFs. In that same year, the report finds total grantmaking from DAFs was less than $35 billion. So, in 2020 alone, the funds would record a net gain of about $12 billion. This is in a year that the National Philanthropic Trust notes was a record setting one for grantmaking via DAFs. Thus, this policy decision has, in effect, diverted funds away from nonprofits and created lucrative new business opportunities at for-profit financial services firms.

Clearly, many of the key policy trends and decisions made by governments in past decades have not proven beneficial to nonprofits, no matter how well intentioned. The effect has been an environment that disincentivizes growth, promotes inefficiencies, and picks clear winners and losers, too often along class and race lines.

How might the government sector more constructively engage with nonprofits to better advance their highest purposes and best effectiveness?

BE BETTER PARTNERS IN PROVIDING SERVICES BY STREAMLINING PROCUREMENT AND PAYING BILLS ON TIME

As discussed in the chapter on nonprofit funding streams, governments are notoriously slow in paying their bills. It is not unusual to wait months or even years after the payments are due to receive them. This is not a new practice. An article in the *Chronicle of Philanthropy* highlights this issue going back to the 2000s in Illinois.

Similarly, the procurement processes to get a government contract in the first place are often complex, require the use of archaic systems, and have long waiting periods. As I am writing this book, I am also eagerly awaiting a state government to issue a Request for Proposals (RFP) that my contacts in the government expected to drop four months ago.

This inefficiency creates two-fold problems. First, it locks up resources for nonprofits who essentially must make interest free loans to the government, reducing their ability to invest in other programs or services. Second, it makes it more difficult for smaller start-up nonprofits to access this revenue stream. Although they may have deeper community ties or more innovative ideas, these small organizations likely lack financial reserves to weather long delays in payment or the staff capacity to navigate long, complex RFP requirements.

At a high level, Congress and state legislatures should create policies that incentivize executive branch departments to pay their bills timely and create consequences for those that fail to do so. Furthermore, action should be taken to streamline and modernize procurement processes generally. This could happen within the executive branch or through legislative action. Finally, to be truly equitable, such modernizations could take a differentiated approach that offers simplified or expedited processes for smaller or start-up nonprofits, particularly those from disadvantaged or underserved communities.

SUPPORT NONPROFITS IN TAKING A SEAT AT THE TABLE IN POLICY DISCUSSIONS IMPACTING THE SECTOR AND ITS WORK

Although they have broad rights to do so, many 501(c)(3) nonprofits are highly circumspect about engaging in policy advocacy activities, from meeting with legislators to mobilizing grassroots activists. When they do so, it is often cautiously and generally in service to their missions. And, as is becoming my refrain, having greater resources creates greater capacity. The result is that, even in issues directly concerning the sector, nonprofits have little to no voice.

Into this vacuum come rushing other interests eager to take advantage of opportunities to redesign the tax code or otherwise influence policymaking. It must be acknowledged that redesigning the policy process as we know it is likely not an attainable goal. However, there is plenty of room for the government to do more to encourage nonprofits to take their rightful place in that process.

The Internal Revenue Service could use its rulemaking authority to further clarify and better articulate the advocacy rights of 501(c)(3) nonprofits in simply reframing the administrative structure for nonprofits to frame advocacy as a positive right, rather than a risky gray area. Something as dry as the tax code could play an essential role in creating a fairer landscape for nonprofits without even significantly changing existing rules. As long as nonprofits remain unable to confidently participate in the policy process, we are unlikely to see outcomes favorable to their interests.

LEVERAGE THE VAST VOLUME OF DATA AND ACCESS IT HAS TO CHAMPION PROMISING PRACTICES AND PROVIDE USEFUL DATA TO THE PUBLIC

The IRS and state governments can, and do, compel nonprofits to produce vast volumes of data. They use tools like the Form 990 Informational Return, which all tax-exempt organizations are required to submit on annually (Internal Revenue Service 2021). Most state governments also have annual state charitable solicitation filings as well. This information is made freely available to the public, including as downloadable data files.

However, in its current form, the data is largely inscrutable, both to policymakers and ordinary citizens. Many organizations and experts who analyze the nonprofit sector use this data. However, those organizations are doing so to advance their own agenda, and they often put their findings behind a "paywall." Policymakers should ensure that it is being used, not just warehoused. Policymakers should invest in ensuring that executive departments capturing such data are storing it in ways that facilitate analysis.

Furthermore, they should provide summary reporting on the state of the nonprofit sector in service to the public good and make it publicly available regularly. Doing so would create better insight into the needs of the sector and even create opportunities to identify and resolve problems earlier in their development. A shift from passive data collection and warehousing to active engagement and analysis would allow both policymakers and citizens to be more effective partners.

The nonprofit sector doesn't thrive or struggle in a vacuum. The policy choices that the federal, state, and, in some cases, local governments make have a clear impact on the ability of the sector to be equitable, innovative, and efficient. The present, overall approach to government engagement with the nonprofit sector does not serve either group particularly well. There are some bright spots, like Colorado's legislation making it easier for citizens to direct their tax refund dollars to charitable organizations.

The overall picture is one of a policy landscape that stifles competition, disincentivizes innovation, and disadvantages many nonprofits in favor of a small number of very large, well-established organizations. For the nonprofit sector to effectively fulfill its role, and to ensure the goals of having a nonprofit tax-exempt sector robust in helping meet the needs in communities for the common good and effectively partner with other parts of civil society, a new approach is needed. Embracing these new policy directions would be a significant step forward in achieving such a reset.

PART 3

CHAPTER 7

The Special Relationship: Connections between Donors and Nonprofits

---

The relationship between donors and nonprofits they fund is one of the most important in keeping the nonprofit sector thriving. However, a philanthropic gift can also be fraught with more complicated, underlying needs and emotions. Afterall, we aren't buying a burrito or a new coffee maker; while the price might be similar, the impact of the exchange is very different. As discussed in the chapter on the history and evolution of nonprofits, this is likely because of the deep cultural and moral roots that helped to shape our modern nonprofit sector and still color relationships in it.

On the other side of the transaction, many nonprofits face what can feel like a paradox. They should be focused on fulfilling their missions, but to do that they need the support of donors. Donors with their own needs, priorities, and expectations. In some cases, there is a natural alignment between the donors who support the organization and the clients it serves. But, for many organizations, donors and beneficiaries are two disparate groups. Hence, the paradox: How can the staff and volunteers at a nonprofit stay mission focused while also effectively engaging donors to ensure needed funds are raised?

Clearly, there is money to be made in trying to help both sides to manage this complex but essential relationship, and unsurprisingly plenty of for-profit companies have emerged to fill the void. For donors, particularly wealthy ones, there is no shortage of experts to advise them on how to make the "right" philanthropic contributions or set the best "giving strategy." On the other side, we have a multitude of consultants, strategists, and advisors coaching nonprofits, particularly the big ones, on how to engage and activate donors most effectively. While many of these folks can offer great insight and bring a lot of sophistication to their respective work, ultimately, they benefit from complexity and division. After all, if this work was easy and straightforward, there wouldn't be a need for their services.

They aren't totally self-serving, though. As this book has shown, the nonprofit sector is large, diverse, and can be incredibly powerful. It can also be complex, and making savvy decisions about how to invest in nonprofits can be daunting. I've met with many donors in various settings, from offices to cocktail parties to Amtrak's Northeast Regional. I've also made cold calls, sent direct mail appeals, and planned Instagram influencer campaigns to raise money.

I've also been a donor to plenty of nonprofits myself. In my experience, much like nonprofits, the vast majority of donors are deeply sincere in their desire to have a positive impact on society and try to make good decisions about causes to support.

This chapter aims to cut through the noise and share some principles I use as a nonprofit insider when making decisions about my own donations as well as some insights of what I view as effective strategies for fundraising. My goal here is merely to provide food for thought to donors and insiders as they consider their own giving decisions and design their own fundraising efforts. I hesitate to call them rules, because I think in a sector as big and complex as American nonprofits, very few rules are absolutes. I see them more as gut checks or guidelines.

GUIDANCE FOR DONORS

POLISHED DOESN'T MEAN POWERFUL

Remember that a polished fundraising appeal doesn't necessarily equal powerful impact. In many cases it just means the organization has invested a lot of resources in building a sophisticated fundraising program. Don't get me wrong, we all love a beautiful handwritten thank you note or birthday card. Running a high-end fundraising operation requires lots of personalization, customization, party planning, video production, and detailed tracking of interests, preferences, and personal details. All that activity is expensive and time intensive. How long it takes an organization to send you a tax receipt has very little to do with the quality of their programs and a lot more to do with how many hours of staff time they have dedicated to donor acknowledgments. As a nonprofit professional, I encourage my colleagues in the sector to invest the time and money required to be timely and respectful in their engagement with donors.

However, doing so doesn't make a nonprofit's programs more effective or impactful. Donors should not read too much into the personalization of solicitations or the quality of the canapes at a donor reception. Many donors I've talked to complain that nonprofits "waste" too much money on fundraising and courting them, while simultaneously giving most generously to organizations that invest the most in fundraising, thus creating perverse incentives.

In relying too heavily on the quality of the "donor experience" in making giving decisions, a donor can end up perpetuating unjust systems. Many of the rules of excellent donor experience favor larger, older, and (more often than not) white-led organizations over those who have had less opportunity to acquire the resources to create those elite experiences.

DO YOUR OWN HOMEWORK

There are well over a million nonprofits operating at any given time, and new ones receive their IRS determination letters every day. One of the great strengths of the nonprofit sector is its dynamic, flexible, innovative nature. However, this can present a challenge to those who are eager to create "rules" and standard metrics to tell a citizen whether an organization is well-run or effective. That hasn't stopped the emergence of a cottage industry of experts in academia, for-profit consultants, and (of course) nonprofits that specialize in trying to do just that. The reality is, particularly if you are considering a large or long-term investment in a nonprofit, there is no substitute for doing your own due diligence.

The various rating sites, giving guides, and expert briefs are absolutely tools that can help you in your effort to learn. But it is important to read organizational materials, review documents, and (if possible) ask your own questions to develop your own understanding and form your own judgment. This is true for a few reasons. First, any ratings system or listing has some arbitrariness built in. At Charity Navigator, for example, they had to pick a cut off for each element of the score, particularly on the financial side. Is a nonprofit that spends on average $0.22 to raise a dollar meaningfully less efficient than one that spends $0.20 to raise a dollar? Probably not. However, that difference could be the deciding factor between a four-star and a three-star rating for a nonprofit (Charity Navigator 2022).

I share this not to cast aspersions on raters—they are after all just trying to build consistent evaluative tools. Rather, my aim is to highlight the inherent incompleteness and arbitrariness of these rating systems. Second, since the sector is so broad and diverse, it can be difficult to know which metrics are most relevant to a given organization without understanding its model and goals. Finally, and most importantly, only by conducting your own research can you figure out how well the organization's operations fit with your personal values and truly establish trust in their mission and management.

SEEK OUT AND INVEST IN NONPROFITS WALKING THE TALK

Give to nonprofits that consistently operate in alignment with their own mission, vision, and values. Many donors spend time learning about an organization's mission, its clients, or its goals, keeping the focus on the external. However, far fewer spend time understanding the way the organization operates, how it treats its staff, or the composition of its board—the intangibles that make up its organizational ethos.

However, in my experience, the condition of the internal operations of an organization can provide essential insights into the true condition and level of impact of its external programs. I once worked as a consultant at an organization that was extremely loose in its approach to compliance. Required state charitable solicitation licenses went unrenewed until the second or third warning, audits were delayed then canceled, and IRS forms were filed only after the last possible extension had lapsed. Thus, it was not surprising to me when the board learned that a leadership staff member had been significantly misusing program funds for months, leaving more junior staff unpaid and seriously damaging the program's reputation.

If you want to understand the true quality and impact of an organization, pay attention to the details of how things operate behind the scenes.

GIVE WITH THE FEWEST RESTRICTIONS AND COMMIT FOR THE LONG TERM

If you trust and respect a nonprofit, prioritize giving unrestricted gifts consistently year after year. Unrestricted gifts allow greater flexibility, reduce the burden on organizations, and generally allow the money to have more impact because less of it is spent on recordkeeping and reporting. Additionally, since most nonprofits face a constantly shifting mosaic of funds, points of consistency in the funding stream allow the nonprofit to spend less time seeking new donors and dollars and, instead, devote those resources to bold goals. If you are concerned that the organization may not use your funds responsibly or ethically, you may want to spend more time learning about them or reflecting on whether the organization aligns with your values.

If your goal is to commemorate your family or celebrate a milestone, there are plenty of symbolic forms of recognition and celebration that don't require locking funds into highly specialized programs or creating onerous reporting requirements.

MAKE GIVING JOYOUS

Contributing your money or time to a nonprofit is, fundamentally, an act of hope. Hope that their mission will be fulfilled, their vision will be achieved, and our collective community will beenriched. Try not to lose sight of that when considering how to engage with the nonprofit sector. Embrace the fun of making a bet on the future. Take pleasure in doing your small part in mending the world.

Nonprofits confront many complex, persistent, and poorly understood problems. At the end of the day, it is highly unlikely that any one solution is fundamentally the "best." In the face of this complexity, I embrace equifinality. Or, less pretentiously, I believe that there is more than one way to skin a cat. So give your resources in good faith, in accordance with your ethics and best judgment. Chances are good that even if you aren't giving to whichever nonprofit is the "best" or most highly rated or largest, you will make a positive difference.

I hope these principles serve as a flexible guide to help readers feel confident in becoming donors of their time, talent, and treasure to nonprofits. They have helped me in making many decisions about my own giving and are informed by my experiences on both sides of the sector.

On the other side of the divide, how can those of us in the nonprofit sector work more effectively to communicate with and engage those who are committed to our causes as donors, volunteers, and concerned citizens? I would propose the following five principles to be more effective and productive in your engagement with the community.

GUIDANCE FOR NONPROFIT PROFESSIONALS

LIVE YOUR MISSION AND VALUES CONSISTENTLY
Nothing is more damaging to trust in an institution than a perception of hypocrisy about its values or purpose. This is doubly true in the nonprofit sector, where our ideas about charity and its religious roots still strongly color many

Americans' perceptions of how organizations should operate. High profile nonprofit scandals get the lion's share of attention. However, in my experience, it is the small, everyday bits of hypocrisy that can do damage to an organization's perceived credibility and trust in its work. It's the organization that promotes women's health while not offering paid maternity leave to its staff, or that touts a commitment for diversity on its website as the board remains all white year after year.

These small moments are often subtle, and the elements of hypocrisy can be ambiguous. Decisions that erode organizational integrity are often heralded by one of a few signal phrases, like: "What choice do we have?" or "Think of all of the good this will do," or "Everyone else does it; this is standard practice." Accepting that generous gift from a questionable organization looking to "charity-wash" its image or cutting benefits for staff to make the organization more "sustainable" might feel like the best or only choice. But in the end, the risk to organizational trust outweighs the reward. In the long run, consistency in applying your values across all stakeholder groups from beneficiaries, to staff, to donors will result in a healthier, more effective organization.

TELL COMPLEX STORIES CLEARLY

Storytelling is a powerful tool to rally support and build a movement. It is one of the fundamental ways that we humans connect. I strongly encourage all nonprofit leaders to tell stories as a way of communicating their missions. Many of the strongest organizational leaders are there because they are great storytellers.

However, in the effort to leverage storytelling as a tool, some nonprofits can oversimplify, losing the richness and complexity that ultimately makes stories resonate. The work of the nonprofit sector is often complex and messy, from the highs and lows of the creative process for a theater company to the nuanced work of addiction recovery. The stories from our sector feature enough twists and turns to give any bestselling thriller a run for its money. The casts of characters are often large, with many subplots and bit players.

Too often, I think those trying to tell stories about nonprofits and their work are over-eager to gloss over all this depth in favor of fitting the copy onto a single postcard or just one thirty second Instagram video. The logic often runs along the lines that "people have short attention spans," or people need brevity, simplicity, and easy morals. The result reduces the messy realities of the nonprofit world to tightly packaged, often repetitive fables. In my opinion, rubbing off the rough edges to simplify and compress nonprofit stories does a disservice to both the stories and sector.

First, it can be disrespectful to the people these stories are told about. No one wants to be reduced to a caricature or a stereotype, even if it is a good one. In the quest for brevity, we run the risk of depriving the characters in our stories of their humanity. Many of the most memorable characters in literature are ambiguous and complex, from Hamlet to Anansi. After all, the classic narrative structure of the hero's journey has fourteen steps (Campbell 2008). Humans across time and culture aren't scared of complex stories. The stories just need to be told well with clarity and honesty.

I encourage my fellow nonprofit professionals to embrace radical honesty in storytelling. They should resist the urge to oversimplify or overdramatize. Often donors or community members can see themselves in the most unexpected parts of a story. This can be true for visual storytelling as well.

I once worked at a nonprofit whose focus was serving new parents. This nonprofit did head-to-head testing of two types of images for a fundraising campaign. One set of images was straight out of Hollywood—pristinely clean children in cute outfits frolicking in the park. A mom with immaculate hair and makeup reading a story to an attentive toddler. The other set captured the mundane, quotidian aspects of parenthood. A new mother breastfeeding on the toilet, a crying toddler in the park, a dad with spit-up on his shirt. Nothing terribly bleak or dramatic—just the day-to-day, less than perfect things parents experience. The campaign that performed better was the one that portrayed the "real" experience of parenthood.

I believe by telling stories that are realistic, nuanced, and well-structured, nonprofits can more authentically and respectfully connect with the public and inspire support.

ENGAGE WITH ALL STAKEHOLDERS RESPECTFULLY AND INTENTIONALLY

Too often nonprofits are excessively deferential to some groups while completely ignoring others. Can you imagine chiding a donor for being late to a meeting or missing a deadline? I know I can't. But, for a program participant in a homelessness program, such treatment is routine or even expected. This is a problem. Not only is it unfair and unkind, but it reinforces hierarchies, discourages a sense of shared identity between groups, and ultimately erodes trust. People in each group are likely to notice the differences, and it can build resentment. Inconsistent behavior can cause individuals to question the organization's authenticity.

NURTURE AND DEVELOP TALENT WITHIN THE SECTOR
As we have learned throughout the book, the nonprofit sector is distinctive, and understanding its distinctions takes time. The more the nonprofit can build a corps of committed professionals who understand the ways the sector plays a unique role, the more the sector can build trust with others both within and outside of the sector. Doing so will require a commitment to creating pathways for people who pursue nonprofit careers to have sufficient financial support to do so, meaningful opportunities for advancement, and the chance to feel challenged and valued. Implementing this principle means a commitment to all the things that make the nonprofit sector unique and different from government or the for-profit sector.

BE A CHAMPION FOR ALL NONPROFITS
Resources for nonprofits are often tight, and competition for the biggest grants, most generous contracts, or prime partnerships can be fierce. However, at the end of the day, the millions of organizations in the nonprofit sector are profoundly interdependent. We should stick up for each other and advocate for the sector, not just whichever organizations happen to employ us or the cause that we are most

passionate about. There is something to be said for solidarity and acknowledging that a tide can lift all boats, particularly when it comes to public policy issues. Nonprofits can play a powerful role in advocating for policies that support the sector as well as create better experiences for their clients.

When nonprofits operate with leaders who have a mindset of competition, the temptation to criticize other organizations or positions given as a zero-sum game can be overwhelming. If donors are pulled into this, it can create distrust in the organizations that are criticized and ultimately the sector. Operating from an approach of abundance and solidarity will instead increase trust.

I sincerely believe that, if broadly implemented, these principles could do much to support more productive engagement between donors and nonprofits, both at the organizational level and across the sector. However, I also acknowledge that there are significant practical barriers to achieving that vision. For example, it would be great if every potential donor to a nonprofit had the time, capacity, and tools to do thoughtful, personal research and due diligence. But that is simply not feasible, particularly for those who have more limited resources to dedicate to philanthropy.

A misalignment of interests exists between all the individuals and firms who earn profits as consultants bridging this divide and the two groups on either side of the divide. These firms have a direct interest in maintaining the present *status quo* for their own benefit. These are significant barriers. To build a more constructive model for engagement between these two interdependent groups, it will be necessary to find a structure that is scalable and where the interests of all parties are better aligned toward a shared outcome.

CHAPTER 8

Trust But Verify: A Case for a Nonprofit Accreditation Model

Nonprofits are central to the functioning of civil society in the United States; they have a long history of providing essential functions that augment and expand the services that government or the private sector can effectively offer. In some cases, nonprofits can be the sole providers of services, for example driving research in rare diseases or, as we saw earlier, connecting victims of intimate partner violence with essential services. Nonprofits can also be drivers of innovation. They offer a flexible, low-barrier structure for concerned citizens to come together and address challenges or bring enhancements to their communities. For all these reasons, nonprofits also attract significant investment to the tune of hundreds of billions of dollars in donations alone. The sector is also a major employer, with tens of millions of staff who work at well over a million nonprofit organizations. For all these reasons, a thriving, efficient nonprofit sector is clearly desirable in the United States.

However, the relationship between nonprofits and citizens is more than just pragmatic. Nonprofits occupy a particular space in the American psyche. They are a manifestation of some of our most generous and communal impulses to care for our neighbors and contribute to the common good. Many nonprofits have ties to diverse faith traditions or are deeply woven into the stories of emigration, adaptation, and growth. Many schools, health systems, and social services agencies still retain these ties in their names and branding. Think of New York Presbyterian or Cedars-Sinai hospitals, or even the Red Cross. These ties go deeper than just branding. They touch the governance structures and policies at the core of these organizations. As a result, many Americans have a different relationship with nonprofits than they would have with other, for-profit corporations.

They have different expectations for transparency, thrift, and ethical decision making for nonprofits. Americans expect nonprofits to be standard bearers for more egalitarian communal values, and to represent our best selves in a way that clearly echoes these roots. Nonprofits face a higher bar to earn and keep public trust and often stronger and more enduring backlash when it is lost. The public experiences collective shock—a deeper sense of injury and indignation when confronted with a corrupt nonprofit CEO. Further, the impacts of stories of scandal and corruption tend to echo more broadly, tarring the whole sector with the same brush.

To maximize its contributions to the health and success of American civil society, the nonprofit sector needs to be trusted, efficient, equitable, and innovative. Embracing these seemingly competing values is a difficult balancing act itself. Unfortunately, the nonprofit sector faces several distinct challenges in doing so, including:

- The distorting effects of mega-donors and their priorities;
- Governance structures that tend to reinforce and amplify social inequalities;
- Systems of funding that favor larger, more established nonprofits, which stifles modernization and innovation; and
- The corrosive effect of a saturated media environment where the misdeeds of the few impact the reputation of the many.

I am certainly not the first author to highlight these issues, and many donors, concerned citizens, and nonprofit professionals have proposed a wide range of solutions to this challenge. We have seen a proliferation of efforts to address each of these elements, some of which have been highlighted in earlier chapters of this book. Many of these solutions focus on aspects of the necessary nonprofit value system. For example, the proliferation of nonprofit ratings tools from Candid's GuideStar to Charity Navigator focus primarily on efficiency and trust, operating on the hypothesis that by requiring certain data be made public and evaluated against collective standards, they can instill trust and prove the efficiency of participating nonprofit organizations.

In the absence of coordinated self-regulation in the nonprofit sector, policymakers at the state level have worked to create more regulatory requirements for disclosure and transparency. Government mandated tools, like more thorough charitable registration processes and public, searchable databases of registered nonprofits and their data, have become more common.

Finally, many academic partners have invested in trying to drive both innovation and efficiency through the creation of specialized centers and enhanced academic research into nonprofits, the problems they aim to solve, and the philanthropy that funds them. Notable examples include the Lilly School of Philanthropy at the University of Indiana and the Center for High Impact Philanthropy at the University of Pennsylvania. Fellowship programs and other efforts to make the sector more equitable and inclusive are also common with notable programs like the National Urban Fellows placing dozens of qualified, diverse leaders committed to racial equity into positions of influence in nonprofits every year.

Mega-donors have also pumped billions into frameworks around innovation and efficiency, from the collective impact fad of the 2000s, to the current trend of "big bet" philanthropy led by entities like the Blue Meridian Partners and the MacArthur Foundation, which are dedicated to making large investments to "scale" innovative programs.

Unfortunately, collectively these solutions have not secured strong trust in the nonprofit sector (see previous chapter for citation about studies of trust), nor have they demonstrated any measurable success in ensuring that nonprofits grow more inclusive or equitable.

ARE THESE EFFORTS EFFECTIVE?

As discussed earlier, the senior leadership teams and boardrooms at nonprofits remain dominated by older, straight white men. In some cases, the collection of efforts by nonprofits, policymakers, and other civil society actors has proven to be counterproductive with progress toward one aim while nullifying progress on others. Most obviously, the many efforts to increase trust in nonprofits through transparency has, in some cases, served to worsen inequity in the sector and stifle innovation.

As state requirements have become more stringent, and the number of topflight external ratings that are *de rigueur* for a credible nonprofit have multiplied, so has the time and complexity of complying with them. These demands place smaller, newer nonprofits, those with less funding, and those experimenting with new programs or theories of impact at a disadvantage. The result is that the nonprofit sector, even as it faces greater demands from complex challenges like pandemic disease and climate change, continues to struggle to maximize its positive impact for society despite the significant efforts and resources invested to try to align, strengthen, and communicate both its value and values. The opportunity cost of this current state is the option to invest those resources directly into the programs and services the sector provides, making the ineffective or even counterproductive nature of these efforts particularly frustrating.

The nonprofit sector is large and complex, and it encompasses a diversity of missions. It is also dynamic and growing with new nonprofits forming and established nonprofits dissolving every year. The National Center for Charitable Statistics estimates that in the decade between 2006 and 2016, the total number of active nonprofits in the United States increased by 60,000.

Based on this current state, it is clear there is room to develop new ways of defining, communicating, and holding nonprofits accountable. It remains essential to determine which nonprofits are effectively fulfilling their core role in the social fabric as trusted, equitable service providers who operate efficiently with the resources entrusted to them by the public and incubate innovation in service to their missions. Fortunately, since there are so many current initiatives in place, there is rich data to evaluate in understanding what characteristics a new initiative would need to maximize its chances for success. Those characteristics include:

1. A holistic perspective;
2. A flexible framework; and
3. An eye toward efficiency.

One of the problems with current efforts to bolster the sector and its perceived value is the narrow focus on only one or two facets of the larger value proposition for the nonprofit sector, thus leaving essential elements out of the equation.

Due to its unique history, place in the culture, and defining structure, the corporation, the nonprofit sector faces a complex set of expectations. To maximize impact, both individual nonprofits, and the nonprofit sector collectively, must aim to: optimize operational efficiency; embrace diversity, equity, and inclusion; retain high levels of public trust; and drive innovation. In practice, this is a balancing act that would give even a seasoned tightrope walker vertigo.

An initiative that boosts trust at the expense of efficiency or enhances innovation without ensuring equity does little to advance a nonprofit's standing or the effectiveness of the sector. Thus, any successful approach to bolstering the sector must be able to clearly address and advance all four facets of the value proposition, both for the sector as a whole and for individual organizations.

WHAT MIGHT WORK BETTER?
To be relevant and effective in this context, any new approach needs a simple, clear, and adaptable framework to define, measure, and contextualize any given nonprofit's contribution to the overall value proposition of the sector.

Such a flexible framework would likely need to be rooted in universal principles aligned with each element of the value proposition that could be operationalized using several different proxies suited to the context of a particular nonprofit or sub-set of nonprofits within the sector. For example, within the value of efficiency the principle of good financial stewardship, which could then be measured by a few more specific measures, like number of operating reserves on hand where the "reference" or target value was set based on the sub-sector the organization identified with.

This kind of framework avoids the pitfall of so many current efforts, which tend to either prioritize universality at the expense of being arbitrary or become so specialized as to be impractical as a way of communicating value back to the public at large.

Finally, to be successful, any new approach to defining, measuring, and communicating the nonprofit sector's individual and collective value proposition must not create additional work or expense for any actor in the sector. In fact, it should aim to create efficiencies and savings.

To do otherwise would contradict one of the core values that define the nonprofit sector. A system that requires greater contribution, particularly of time and expertise, is likely to struggle to find broad adoption, particularly in today's already crowded community. To avoid creating new burdens, any new approach must draw from existing resources, activities, and processes within the nonprofit sector.

For example, if data is gathered, it should be harmonized with existing requirements, an optimal new solution would go one step further and create new efficiencies by streamlining processes or eliminating duplicative or irrelevant efforts.

A potential example here would be reducing the number of times and places that the same piece of information is collected, which increases likelihood of error and inconsistency in addition to being more labor-intensive data that must be reported. Not only would a tool or approach that met that goal actively contribute to the overall value proposition it is trying to define, the delta between the current state and the more efficient future state for many nonprofits could provide the means to make such a tool self-sustaining. Essentially, if the tool or approach can create sufficient savings, it could both make the sector stronger and pay for itself, avoiding the need to divert resources away from the missions of individual organizations.

ACCREDITATION SYSTEM

As I scan other sectors for potential solutions that align with the criteria of a holistic approach, flexible framework, and efficiency, one approach that appears consistently is an accreditation system. Accreditation is defined by the Oxford English Dictionary as "the action or process of officially recognizing someone as having a particular status or being qualified to perform a particular activity."

Accreditation systems exist in many industries and professions, from higher education to healthcare and financial services. Notable examples of large scale, well-established accreditation systems include The Joint Commission (JCAHO), an independent nonprofit itself, which offers accreditation at various levels for almost all types of healthcare facilities in the United States, including hospitals, clinical laboratories, and home health providers with the aim of verifying the safety and quality of their services.

JCAHO has been in operation since 1951 and conducts accreditation services for thousands of healthcare providers annually. JCAHO accreditation is often associated with more favorable reimbursement rates from payors and can be a prerequisite to access certain programs and revenue streams.

Obtaining JCAHO accreditation requires a self-evaluation, site visits to the facility by external experts, and independent evaluation of the collective findings (Joint Commission 2022). Although the precise content of these systems varies widely, the general components and purposes of accreditation systems are generally consistent with those outlined for JCAHO across industries and sectors.

In fact, an analysis of accreditation systems in healthcare, science, and engineering compiled by the National Academies found the broadly universal basic components of a comprehensive accreditation system include: a credible accrediting body; a defined set of standards for accreditation; an application process with clear eligibility criteria; a self-evaluation phase; external evaluation including independent data collection; a body that can hear appeals to accreditation decisions; and finally, an ongoing cycle of self and external evaluation to maintain accreditation (Institute of Medicine 2001).

The National Academies also outlined three basic purposes of accreditation systems (Institute of Medicine 2001).

1. First is a "mark of excellence" supplemental to government regulation. Under this purpose, accreditation is an optional step an organization can pursue in hopes of obtaining some market advantage for going above and beyond statutory and regulatory standards.
2. Second is a model whereby an accreditation process substitutes for government regulation, allowing an industry or sector to self-police.
3. Finally, are accreditation systems that can serve as a replacement for participation in certain regulatory

processes, potentially allowing an accredited organization to substitute the accreditation process for a regulatory one.

Based on this understanding of the basic structure and purpose of accreditation systems, a well-designed and effectively managed accreditation system could serve as a holistic, flexible, and efficient tool to define, measure, and communicate how well an individual nonprofit is aligning with the fundamental value proposition of an innovative, efficient, equitable, and trusted portion of the sector.

CHAPTER 9

Elements of a Sector-Wide Accreditation System

———

The foundation for any accreditation system is a clear set of standards and evaluative criteria to determine whether those standards are being met. Since the accreditation process requires both internal and external evaluation, these standards need to be clearly articulated and have explicit operational definitions. They also need to be comprehensive to assess multiple relevant dimensions of the institution under consideration.

For example, my *alma mater* Georgetown University has been accredited as a higher education institution by the Middle States Commission on Higher Education (MSCHE) since 1921. MSCHE explicitly states that it evaluates institutions holistically and has established seven standards that institutions are evaluated against that each address a different domain of the college or university's operations, from governance and ethics to educational quality and continuous improvement (Middle States Commission on Higher Education 2022).

Each standard is supported by detailed operational criteria. For example, Standard II Ethics and Integrity has nine discrete evaluative criteria designed to determine whether the institution is actually operating ethically. This example highlights the way in which an accreditation system's foundational standards can help it to be holistic in its approach by creating a comprehensive and operational framework that acts as a scaffold for assessment.

Further, it sets the stage for the second element of an effective tool, enhancing the impact of the nonprofit sector, **flexibility**.

As outlined above, accreditation systems require a two-step process of internal and external evaluation, including site visits and operational observation, to apply the standards and determine fit to the operational criteria. The inclusion of this much more active evaluative process injects flexibility into the process by allowing the nuance of professional judgment and the added rigor of empirical data to the measurement of organizations.

Continuing the example above, MSCHE has more than 1,100 volunteer peer reviewers who play a role in observing, reviewing documents, and providing feedback on whether and how an institution can comply with each criterion for each standard. This human touch not only adds a degree of expertise to the process, but it also allows the framework to be flexible enough to address more subjective or qualitative standards.

To return to the MSCHE example, under Standard II Ethics and Integrity, the first criteria is "a commitment to academic freedom, intellectual freedom, freedom of expression, and respect for intellectual property rights" (Middle States Commission on Higher Education 2022). While the criteria here is clear and operational, it would be difficult to ascertain compliance simply using a yes or no question or even by reviewing a document.

This is an essential differentiator between a system of accreditation and a rating system and what makes it more relevant to meeting the requirements to strengthen the nonprofit sector.

RATINGS TOOLS VS. ACCREDITATION

Some of the values the sector needs to embody and communicate, while clear enough, require both empirical and qualitative data along with a dose of subjective judgment to really measure and assess. For example, trust or equity and inclusion. Many of us, me included, have worked at organizations that have erudite and compelling statements on diversity or crystal-clear policies about retaliation in cases of harassment that when the rubber hit the road were not worth the pixels required to spell them out on our computer screens.

I can recall another internship at a nonprofit that prided itself on its values around equity and inclusiveness while systematically favoring students from privileged backgrounds in hiring decisions. Conversely, as a gay man I found Georgetown (at least my division) to be a very welcoming and supportive environment despite a raft of written policies at the Catholic, Jesuit institution that in many cases suggested the opposite.

Ratings systems, even rigorous ones, are unlikely to discern the dissonance between the written policies and actual operations. This is why systems of accreditation are superior and better suited to the needs of a diverse, dynamic sector and value propositions that are rooted in qualitative, empirical data and sometimes even subjective judgements.

The final precondition for success in tools to support the nonprofit value proposition is efficiency. On their face, accreditation systems don't seem to meet this condition. As outlined, they are much more involved than a simple ratings system and seem like they would create more labor for nonprofits and a greater burden on the sector as a whole to administer.

However, a closer analysis of the purposes of systems of accreditation reveals the powerful potential they have to streamline and create efficiencies in the sector. As noted in the National Academies' analysis, accreditation systems can function not simply as another "gold star" or market differentiator for organizations eager for competitive advantage, but as a replacement for or alternative to other forms of oversight and regulation (Institute of Medicine 2001).

In the case of nonprofits, this could look like waiving annual state registration requirements for accredited organizations, or at least a streamlined process. An accreditation system that could offer these benefits would represent a huge savings of time and effort for both nonprofits and their regulators and funders. It would also significantly reduce the asymmetric information problem that hampers efficiency in funding and regulatory decisions.

As a nonprofit professional who has submitted his fair share of grant applications, I can personally vouch for the time and effort required to meet "due diligence" requirements that accompany almost any request for funding, state registration, or partnership opportunity. Due diligence materials are documents, reports, or other materials submitted to establish the organization's *bona fides* as a responsible, well-managed organization, even if their content isn't directly relevant to the gift or partnership in question.

Common requests tend to include things like:

- The organization's IRS determination letter;
- Audited financial statements; or
- The annual budget.

Maddeningly, the requirements are often similar, but not quite similar enough, meaning I'm often hunting down a particular policy document or financial report that this state or funder is the first to request this fiscal year. For example, recently a foundation asked to see the minutes from our last four board meetings. Another queried about the average percentage attendance by board members at meetings over the preceding two years.

Additionally, each entity has its own requirements for submitting due diligence materials, whether it is a particular online portal or PDF template. The effort to complete one request is usually modest, requiring at most an hour or two of emails, searching, and uploading. However, many, if not most nonprofits, field dozens or even hundreds of these requests each year. This is compounded by the fact that due diligence is often an ongoing process with updates on financial status required as frequently as quarterly.

The collective burden is meaningful pulling time, expertise, and resources away from mission fulfillment. For smaller nonprofits with fewer resources, which are more likely to be led and based in communities of color, this burden can create a catch-22. The organization needs funding to expand their staff and capacity, but without more staff and capacity, they can't secure funding. The opportunity to complete one biennial or triennial process of evaluation, review, and accreditation, even a rigorous one, in place of these smaller ongoing requests could represent a significant savings for nonprofits.

A GLUT OF WASTED INFORMATION

So, what do funders or government agencies do with all of this information once they have it?

Fortunately, I have also had the opportunity to experience being on the receiving end of all this documentation. When I lived in Chapel Hill, North Carolina, I had the honor of being selected to serve on the town's Human Services Advisory Board. This board was primarily responsible for implementing a grantmaking process to support human services agencies that were providing resources and services to town residents.

As a recent graduate with a background in public health, this seemed like a dream opportunity. I will admit, my enthusiasm for the role dimmed a bit when I arrived at the town hall for orientation. After being formally sworn into the role, I was rather unceremoniously handed a cardboard banker's box full of paper, printed copies of dozens of grant applications that the committee was tasked with reviewing. (Horrifyingly, the nonprofits had been required to print these applications themselves and hand deliver them to the town hall!)

I would need to adopt a rigorous reading schedule, as each Wednesday evening starting at 5:30 p.m. the board would hold a public hearing to hear from the leaders of five or six of these applicants about their request, ask questions, and offer feedback. Dutifully, I lugged the box home, organized the applications into four massive ring binders by hearing date, and started reading. The applications had to fit a specific template set by the town, and were generally around fifteen pages long and dominated by information about the nonprofit's finances, policies, and evaluation model.

After working my way through the materials for the first hearing, I had a sinking realization—I had no clear idea how I could actually use any of this information to make good decisions on behalf of my fellow citizens as I had so recently sworn to do. In some applications, it was clear that the team preparing the request hadn't understood the prompts and provided confusing or incorrect responses. In others, I lacked the specialized professional knowledge to understand a particular element, but most commonly I lacked the context needed to evaluate a particular claim or compare a data point. As I acclimated to the board, I received the equally reassuring and concerning feedback that I was not alone in this. The process became even more daunting when it came time to review required progress reports on grants made in previous cycles.

That said, the Human Services Advisory Board for Chapel Hill was a volunteer board, composed of citizens selected as much for willingness and availability as any particularly deep expertise. Surely more professional foundations with the benefit of paid staff with deeper experience would be more proficient. However, findings from a study published by Peak Grantmaking, a national association of grantmaking professionals, in 2018 paints an equally grim picture of the utility of all of this carefully gathered information (Bearman 2018). It found that in most cases the foundation staff responsible for collecting the reports struggled to define their purpose.

The study found that the copious data laboriously prepared by nonprofits was almost never used to set strategic directions for funding nor to inform the larger field about promising practices or lessons learned. Most commonly, they cited requiring the reports as an accountability mechanism, or an item "for the files." Only about half of the respondents even identified grant reports as playing a role in future funding decisions about the organization that submitted the report.

The challenges described above are clearly interlocking but, on the surface, puzzling.

WHY ARE NONPROFITS BEING ASKED TO PRODUCE EVER GROWING VOLUMES OF DATA AND DOCUMENTATION FOR THE BENEFIT OF EXTERNAL PARTIES WHO STRUGGLE TO ABSORB AND COMPREHEND IT?

The donors themselves can hardly fail to realize that the burden they are creating is counterproductive. To understand this behavior, it is helpful to consider the donors' actions through the lens of economics and contract theory. Specifically, the principles behind information asymmetry and its impact on markets.

Initially developed by economists, and now widely applied across several disciplines, the fundamental premise is simple: Information asymmetry occurs in transactions where one party to the transaction has more or better information to make their decision (New Palgrave Dictionary of Economics Online Ed. 2021). As a result of this imbalance in information, the parties to the transaction may take actions against their rational, mathematical self-interest. As this happens repeatedly, it can result in negative outcomes overall or even the collapse of a market.

Economists have described and characterized many specific scenarios where asymmetric information creates negative outcomes. One of the most common is adverse selection. In the case of adverse selection, the two parties in the transaction have different information prior to making the transaction, which can cause the transaction itself to be inefficient or simply not to occur. As this process repeats itself, the entire market can freeze or become inefficient. The classic example of this is the case of used car markets, outlined by the Nobel-Prize winning economist George Akerlof.

In his model, buyers in the market for used cars have no clear way to determine whether the used cars are good quality or have hidden problems, so-called lemons. Since buyers have no clear way to gauge the quality of a car, they are unwilling to pay top dollar, driving down the average price in the market. This causes sellers who know that they have good quality cars to exit the market since the prices are lower, meaning a higher proportion of the cars on the market are lemons, perpetuating a destructive cycle (Akerlof 1978).

Obviously, the decision to make a gift to one charity over another is not quite the same as choosing between a 2015 Honda Civic or a 2016 Toyota Camry, but the fundamentals are the same. As an outsider, the prospective donor doesn't have an effective means of differentiating between a "good" nonprofit and one with hidden problems. As a result, they may be unwilling to give to any nonprofit or might only be willing to make a smaller gift. However, the next step in the cycle looks a little different.

As the number of participants in philanthropic giving drops and the total amount donated shrinks or stagnates, nonprofits may seek other sources of revenue such as earned income from fees for service. Alternatively, they may offer fewer or lower quality services or even suspend operations. Rather than the collapse of a market, the result is a reduction in critical services and public goods.

A second common manifestation of information asymmetry that absolutely impacts the nonprofit sector is a scenario known as moral hazard. Moral hazard occurs when risk and reward are decoupled, prompting one party in the transaction to either conceal their true behavior or change their behavior once they are insulated from its risk.

The classic example of this behavior comes from the field of insurance. Once a person becomes insured against a particular risk, their behavior becomes riskier or more careless since they won't bear the cost of the event occurring. This can create problems in the market because it creates incentives for parties to act in riskier ways than would rationally be in their self-interest. It also makes pricing risk difficult. This can ultimately mean that certain actors remove themselves from the market or that the market will generate economically inefficient outcomes (O'Hare 2015).

The key differences between moral hazard and adverse selection have to do with the nature of the information and the timing of its impact.

In moral hazard, the missing information is about the behavior of one of the parties, and its impact is felt after the transaction has occurred. In adverse selection, the missing information is about the fundamental nature of the product or service being offered, and the risk happens before or at the point of the transaction. In nonprofit-funder relationships, moral hazard has to do with the true risk profile of a nonprofit. A donor can't know in advance how "risky" their gift to a nonprofit might be since the nonprofit could change its behavior after securing the gift or could conceal its true behaviors during the application or cultivation process. Much like adverse selection, this missing information could cause a donor to decide not to give at all, to give less generously, or very commonly, to try to impose a large number of restrictions on their gift. The idea of the restrictions is to prevent at least one part of moral hazard, the risk that the organization changes its behavior once it has received the funds.

This last point represents the crux of the issue. Clearly the "market" for philanthropic giving hasn't entirely collapsed. Hundreds of billions of dollars still flow into nonprofits from individuals, foundations, corporations, and government every year. However, the market has stagnated and concentrated. As outlined earlier the book, overall giving has been stuck at around 2 percent of GDP for decades, and the vast majority of contributions accrue to a comparatively small group of generally white-led, larger, and more established organizations. This can likely be attributed to some of the current adaptive behaviors that nonprofits and funders are using to accommodate and overcome the problems created by asymmetric information. Essentially, these behaviors boil down to three things: signaling, screening, and regulation. These behaviors are also drawn from the same contract theory framework that helped to define the asymmetric information scenarios above.

Signaling is behavior by the "seller," in this case nonprofits. The nonprofit is trying to credibly convey information that it self-curated to indicate its quality to the "buyer," in this case funders. The goal is to communicate, albeit indirectly, certain qualities about the organization that a funder would value, such as trustworthiness, effective management, or impact. Essentially, how can a nonprofit indicate that it is "one of the good ones" and not "a scam." One common form this behavior can take is publicly promoting gifts, grants, or contracts from other prestigious funders. This can take the form of donor honor rolls on a website, high profile board members, or even endorsements from influencers on Instagram or YouTube. A good external affairs shop at a nonprofit is constantly signaling the prestige, trustworthiness, and effectiveness of the organization. There is even some empirical evidence that suggests this type of signaling might motivate donor behavior. In a large-scale field test, researchers John List and Dean Karlan found that they could raise more money from small-dollar donors by invoking a matching grant from the Bill & Melinda Gates Foundation than by offering the same match from an anonymous donor (Karlan 2020).

Screening is behavior by a potential "buyer," in this case the donor attempting to gather more information about a potential "seller" to overcome the information gap. This screening can happen directly, as in the case of the extensive grant applications, or indirectly using ratings tools and referrals to make funding decisions. In some cases, specialized firms screen nonprofits. This behavior is very common and deeply embedded into philanthropic culture. If you have ever googled a nonprofit before donating to make sure they weren't in the midst of a scandal, you have engaged in screening behavior. At a more granular level, screening can look like setting standards for certain financial ratios or requiring that nonprofits have a certain number of years of operation to apply for a grant.

Although these behaviors can help compensate for the asymmetry of information between funders and nonprofits, they clearly aren't perfect. First, even with them in place, the market is still not functioning at its optimum. Engaging in these signaling and screening behaviors takes time and money from both donors and nonprofits, resources that could instead be directed toward mission fulfillment. Second, the signals and screening tools can be arbitrary. They rely on the selective use of data to convince two parties to complete a transaction. Frequently, therefore, they rely on heuristics and shorthand tapping into dominant cultural paradigms and beliefs to communicate trustworthiness or exclude the "ineffective" or "scams." This has two common results: inefficient transactions and sector-wide inequity.

Giving transactions can be inefficient from the perspective of the donor and from the perspective of society because the goal of signaling or screening isn't necessarily to provide objective proof about the quality of the investment. There may or may not be any correlation between the filter in the screening system or the signal sent by a nonprofit and the actual goals of a donor in giving. The signal could still be deceptive, or the screening filter could exclude the wrong organizations. To extrapolate from the List and Karlan study, the fact that the Bill & Melinda Gates Foundation had also given to a nonprofit doesn't actually tell us anything about the quality, probity, or effectiveness of the nonprofit. It simply suggests those things by association.

Using heuristics also demonstrates why heavy reliance on these behaviors contributes to the inequities that plague the sector. Heuristics are cognitive shorthand, and in the United

States, shorthand frequently defaults to values and beliefs shaped by white, cis, male perspectives. Access to high profile donors to include on your appeal is often through the closed, exclusive networks of board leadership. Screening criteria for "evidence-based programs" rely heavily on Eurocentric modes of empiricism and evaluation methodologies that can be prohibitively expensive as well as systematically under-representing certain communities. Besides being fundamentally unjust, these biases built into a system dependent on signaling and screening also result in imperfect outcomes because they fail to objectively identify the best transaction.

A well-designed, effectively implemented system of accreditation can help to overcome the challenge of asymmetric information both more efficiently and more effectively than these more organic signaling and screening behaviors because, by design, accreditation systems align behaviors with goals through the application of measurable criteria. Further, the more in-depth assessment process embedded in accreditation makes it more difficult for organizations to rely on shorthand or generic assumptions to pass through the process.

An accreditation system, like any other structure in the United States, would still be vulnerable to integrating classist, racist, ableist, or other prejudices into its criteria and processes. However, there are a few safeguards that are inherent in the design of accreditation systems that could help to mitigate that risk and, ultimately, produce a more equitable system capable of creating better outcomes.

First, accreditation systems are not inherently rivalrous. The fact that another organization is accredited does not diminish the value of my organization's accreditation, and in fact, widespread adoption makes the status more, not less, valuable. This contrasts with many signaling behaviors which rely on access to limited resources like high-profile endorsements, which are more inherently rivalrous. The non-rivalrous nature of accreditation means that the playing field for accessing it is more level since you don't need access to exclusive donors or high-end tools to participate.

Second, accreditation systems are inherently designed to be flexible with room in the system for multiple paths to fulfilling a particular criterion or meeting a standard. They embrace diversity and difference by integrating more deeply nuanced both self and external review processes. Seldom does an accreditation system work in absolutes. This creates the space for a diversity of approaches and philosophies to be endorsed and accredited. For example, under an accreditation system, an organization can design a program evaluation process that is culturally competent for the community and not fear being dinged because they can't report on specific key performance indicators. Ultimately, this would allow for organizations that operate outside a white, Western paradigm greater opportunity to be heard and affirmed.

Third, the accreditation system would be new. An opportunity arises through accreditation to build a new system for defining, measuring, and communicating the value of individual nonprofit organizations and the nonprofit sector on a foundation of equity and inclusion. Since there are no existing, large-scale programs focused on this space, the entire generative process, from initial stakeholder conversations to scaling, could be executed with a strong lens for racial, ethnic, and economic diversity. Naturally, this is not guaranteed. However, as the next chapter will outline, any effort to launch a system that doesn't embrace these principles is unlikely to succeed.

CHAPTER 10

Putting Accreditation into Practice

An accreditation model for nonprofits shows clear promise as a tool to improve the quality of the relationship between civil society, government, and the nonprofit sector. Accreditation would do so by creating a framework for the sector—defining, measuring, and directly communicating the trustworthiness, efficiency, equity, and innovativeness of individual organizations.

Essentially, accreditation could serve as an effective mediator for the essential qualities of enough individual nonprofits to have a collective impact that will strengthen the value proposition of the sector. The holistic approach, flexibility, and efficiency of a system of accreditation also suggests that it could be a more comprehensive, impactful approach to this need, especially when compared to existing tools, like rating systems, high profile endorsements, and increasingly complex academic frameworks.

Achieving the promise of a nonprofit accreditation system hinges substantially on effective implementation. This chapter will explore what a successful implementation might look like, using the principles outlined in the previous chapter as a guide. This chapter cannot be a comprehensive operator's manual for such a significant undertaking. Rather, it is designed to outline some fundamental principles for success and provide food for thought about how they might practically be realized.

A successful accreditation system will need to achieve excellence across the following seven domains to be both sustainable and effective in accomplishing its core purposes:

1. **Authentic Efficiencies**—Participation in accreditation must save time and money for both donors and nonprofits. It could do this by eliminating the need for duplicative due diligence processes from donors and reducing the need for signaling behaviors from nonprofits.
2. **Public Policy Alignment**—Accreditation standards, criteria, and processes should be closely harmonized with government requirements. Any accredited organization must also be in good standing with relevant government regulators like the IRS. It should also harmonize with other relevant accreditation processes where appropriate or necessary (i.e., JCAHO for healthcare, etc.).
3. **Broad Applicability**—The accreditation system must be one that can be used for significant portions of the sector. It needs to be able to accommodate organizations of varying levels of complexity and with diverse missions. Broad applicability also implies that the system is ideologically agnostic. It can't too directly prioritize

a particular worldview, like effective altruism, or it will fail to be broadly accepted by both nonprofits and donors.

4. **Equity**—This must be embedded in multiple dimensions across any accreditation system. First, the system must be designed to avoid privileging larger, more established nonprofits over those with more limited resources. Second, the system must be designed to consider the voices of all stakeholders and avoid giving undue weight to evidence and approaches to evaluation that might be rooted in privilege. Third, obtaining accreditation and participation in the accreditation system should be accessible and inclusive to individuals from a wide range of backgrounds.

5. **Diverse identities**—An effective system needs to embrace diversity in many dimensions. Race, ethnicity, gender, and lived experience are particularly important in my mind. If it is to succeed, the accreditation system must mirror the diversity of the nonprofits it evaluates and the clients they serve. It is particularly significant that this diversity needs to exist at all levels and in all parts of the process. A system built only by the wealthy or those with the benefit of extensive formal post-secondary education is bound to fail to serve the whole sector effectively.

6. **Transparency**—Transparency about the elements of the accreditation process and how they are implemented are essential. While there may need to be some safeguards to protect certain confidential information about individual organizations, in general, anyone who is interested should be able to directly observe the system at work, including essential decision-making processes.

7. **Stakeholder Engagement**—A credible nonprofit accreditation system must include the voices of all relevant

stakeholders in all parts of the accreditation process. These stakeholders would include nonprofit professionals, board members, funders, and those that use the nonprofit sector's products and services. It may also include subject-matter experts and academics.

WHAT ORGANIZATIONAL STRUCTURE IS SUITED TO DESIGN AND SUBSEQUENTLY IMPLEMENT A SYSTEM THAT IS BEST POSITIONED TO ACHIEVE SUCCESS ACROSS THESE SEVEN DOMAINS?

Nonprofits, generally, implement the accreditation systems to which they are subject or to which they apply. Examples include JCAHO and the Association for the Accreditation of Human Research Protection Programs (AAHRPP) in the healthcare space (AAHRPP 2022). This is in addition to the regional educational accreditation bodies. Finally, there are specialty accrediting bodies in IT services like the Electronic Healthcare Network Accreditation Commission (EHNAC) (EHNAC 2022). They all benefit from the flexible corporate structure of nonprofits. The associated options for association structures, combined with the perception of impartiality associated with eliminating profit as motive, are also important selling points. In addition, a nonprofit managed accreditation system would remain nimbler in adapting to changing industry norms and emergent challenges than most government regulatory and rulemaking processes. This insight was also noted in the National Academies' analysis of accreditation systems for healthcare and research (Institute of Medicine 2001).

WOULD A NONPROFIT ACCREDITING BODY WORK AS THE ACCREDITING BODY FOR ITS FELLOW NONPROFITS?

Clearly nonprofits have a track record of success in implementing accreditation systems, so on the surface the answer should be yes. However, the list of domains above includes some areas that are common weaknesses in the nonprofit sector. Notably, many nonprofits struggle to ensure that people from historically disenfranchised communities or those with less social, financial, and political capital are well-represented, especially in senior leadership roles and on their boards.

Further, nonprofits pursuing a balanced funding mix, or even just financial sustainability, are vulnerable to the influence of funders who could make achieving goals around equity and transparency more difficult. Additionally, to obtain the efficiencies necessary to justify the creation of an accreditation system for nonprofits, the system ultimately needs to be able to work not just as a "gold star" but as a replacement for certain due diligence processes and potentially regulatory ones as well. This requires a tremendously high level of trust in the accreditor and the accreditation system. It also requires close collaboration with government agencies at all levels.

Thus, while a nonprofit structure might provide a good foundation for an accrediting body to be successful across all seven domains, it is likely the nonprofit would need to pursue a public-private partnership model, likely in partnership with the federal government. Essentially, to be effective, the accrediting body for nonprofits would need to function as a Quango or Quasi-NGO. Quangos are nongovernmental organizations that have had some governmental functions and authority delegated to them.

Despite their silly names, Quangos generally have a greater degree of autonomy than formal executive departments. However, they also benefit from government resources, including funding or nonfinancial support like office space or supplies. As a balance to the unique authorities and resources they are granted, governments typically reserve the right to make significant appointments to organizational leadership roles and sometimes exercise enhanced oversight (Watts 2003). Under such an arrangement, the accreditation body could likely preserve the more flexible, adaptable corporate structure of a nonprofit while ensuring the kind of transparency and commitment to open access by stakeholders who are hallmarks of good government.

There is precedent for using such a model in similar settings, and examples of longstanding "Quango-style" public private partnerships include Fannie Mae and Freddie Mac in mortgage lending, the Voice of America in media, and Boards of Nursing at the state level. These organizations, some of which have been in operation for close to a century, could provide a blueprint for the structure of an accreditation body for nonprofits.

WHO WILL PAY FOR THE SYSTEM OF ACCREDITATION?
Like many nonprofits, the accrediting body would be prudent to fund itself through multiple discrete revenue streams. Maintaining multiple revenue streams would both insulate the accrediting body from potential shocks and disruptions

and protect its independence by making it more difficult for any single donor, funder, or consumer to gain undue leverage. The natural sources of funding would be the critical stakeholders and beneficiaries of the system: nonprofits, private funders, and the government. It would be both logical and desirable for all three groups to contribute to the financing of an accrediting body. However, there are three key considerations essential to ensuring that the funding of the organization doesn't compromise its effectiveness.

First, funds from private philanthropy should be accepted on a strictly fee-for-service basis. In other words, the accrediting body should not accept donations. It should offer services and benefits for sale instead. Keeping the relationship with private philanthropy strictly transactional would reduce the possibility that any donor could exert excessive influence. It would also drastically reduce the possibility of rent-seeking behavior on the part of major philanthropies hoping to influence the accreditation system or process.

Second, fees charged to nonprofits seeking accreditation should be based on a sliding scale that considers at minimum organizational size and complexity in setting prices. This would help ensure the system could be broadly accessible to a large selection of the nonprofit sector. Given the importance of building equity into the system, it would also make sense to create mechanisms to reduce or eliminate fees for nonprofits led by or serving marginalized and underrepresented groups in the nonprofit sector, like Black or Indigenous communities.

Third, while government support is desirable, the source and nature of that support is relevant. Some sources of government support, like a budget line item, are more likely to be subjected to the vicissitudes of the policymaking process. This could make the consistent operation and implementation of a system for accreditation difficult.

In considering a public funding stream, an accrediting body would be wise to take a two-pronged approach to managing risk. First, they should attempt to mitigate exposure to the political process in accessing funding. It is not possible to completely divorce public funding from politics. In considering a public funding stream, an accrediting body would be wise to take a two-pronged approach to managing risk. First, they should attempt to mitigate exposure to the political process in accessing funding. It is not possible to completely divorce public funding from politics. However, not all forms of funding have equal exposure to politics. For example, a grant program through the executive branch has less exposure than does a multi-year appropriation than does a single-year appropriation. Second, the proportion of funding derived from public dollars should be modest and balanced with the other revenue streams so that dips or delays in funding wouldn't preclude the organization from operating.

WHO SHOULD HELP TO CREATE THIS NEW SYSTEM? HOW SHOULD WE SELECT THEM?

To succeed in developing the system equitably, the process for selecting the leaders tasked with building the system must be transparent, accessible, balanced, and inclusive. As discussed in the chapter on boards of directors, far too often positions of power and responsibility in the nonprofit sector are only available through informal networks that tend to require a great deal of privilege to access. It is worth noting that in recent years a greater focus on diversity, equity, and inclusion has led to a gradual increase in the number of women and people of color selected to participate. To ensure that trend continues, the selection process for the group of staff and volunteers to build the accreditation system would need to be open and transparent.

It is also important that the community building the accreditation system should represent all the key stakeholders in the nonprofit sector: nonprofit professionals, program beneficiaries, funders, and government. To be credible and trusted, it is essential that all of these groups feel their needs and priorities are fairly considered in the development process.

POTENTIAL DOMAINS FOR THE ACCREDITATION PROCESS:
Although a system of accreditation would ultimately need to be built by a diverse and inclusive group, as outlined above, I offer the following potential domains for consideration: differentiating it from other forms of accreditation or inspection in which some nonprofits already participate.

1. Operational Efficiency—Covers the organization's allocation of financial, human, and other resources in service to its mission. Does the organization have the right policies, processes, and people in place to ensure its investments are aligned with its purpose?

2. Financial Stewardship—Is record keeping and management sound? Does the organization keep clear records, in a timely manner about how it earns and spends money? Is it authentically engaging in financial oversight processes like audits?
3. Community Alignment—Is the organization structured in such a way that it can regularly receive input and feedback from the various communities it serves? Does its financial model, governance structure, and service delivery allow for it to be responsive to the needs of the people who surround it geographically, support it, or depend on its services?
4. Equity—How does the organization ensure its actions are just and fair to all stakeholders? Does the organization have diverse representation on decision-making bodies? Does it have processes to identify disparate impacts from decisions? Are people empowered to enact change when disparate impacts are discovered?
5. Good Governance—This is all about ensuring a strong board. Although the board and its operations may be relevant across multiple domains, it is important to have policies, procedures, and practices that ensure the organization is well governed.
6. Impact and Evaluation—What is the organization's approach to determining whether it is effectively serving its exempt purpose, and is it sound? Are resources dedicated to collecting feedback, analyzing data, and responding to lessons learned? Although evaluation can take many forms, it is important that organizations have mechanisms to analyze, reflect, and act on changes that can help them best serve their exempt purposes.

These suggested domains focus less on technical expertise or checking compliance requirements for a given technical area, as more specialized forms of accreditation might. Instead, they focus on discerning alignment between an organization's practices and the hallmarks of trusted, stable, and efficient nonprofits. In this way, this broader nonprofit accreditation avoids duplicating other more service area specific systems of accreditation.

WHAT ARE THE LIMITS OF ACCREDITATION?
Although a broadly implemented system of accreditation could offer significant benefit to nonprofits, the nonprofit sector, and ultimately civil society, it is not a panacea. It is a powerful tool, and one that could advance the sector significantly. However, there are other forces and barriers at play.

Nonprofits will still face the distorting effects of mega-donors and the concentration of wealth in donor advised funds and foundations with low or no payout requirements. That is a problem that requires a different public policy fix. In addition, accreditation is, by its very nature, a slow-moving deliberative process. Even once the system is conceived and launched, accreditation cycles tend to span multiple years. Thus, while successful implementation could drive profound positive shifts, these shifts are likely to take place on the scale of years and decades. An analysis of healthcare nonprofits that completed accreditation processes via the Council on Accreditation affirms that this is also true in practice. The organizations studied did see improvements in service delivery, but the timeframe required was generally around three years (Carman 2014). There are likely to be more timely and easier to implement changes that should be put into place alongside the model of accreditation.

A strong system of accreditation can help streamline significant burdens in the relationship between a nonprofit and its other stakeholders, but there are certain things it can't address. Nor can it provide perfect information. For example, questions of personal values and specific questions about the impact and effectiveness of a given organization or intervention. Accreditation would simply establish a foundation of trust in the basic quality of the organization. There could still be a need to do more specialized assessments, particularly for nonprofits that operate in highly technical spaces. I am not suggesting this accreditation model could replace JCAHO accreditation for nonprofit hospitals. But it could still alleviate a significant burden on that hospital's foundation.

Finally, the practical and resource barriers to successful implementation are meaningful. Building a just, effective, and broadly implemented system of accreditation will require sustained investment of financial and political capital. It will mean building and managing coalitions across sector, professional, and interpersonal lines over years and decades. The nuances are myriad and the opportunities for the project to fail legion. However, even if it is not fully successful, an effort to establish such a system is still likely to produce benefits in the form of greater investments in nonprofits and new relationships between stakeholders in discrete sectors.

Building a system of accreditation that can be broadly implemented across the nonprofit sector is almost certainly going to be a complex, expensive, and time-consuming process.

However, with goodwill and firm commitment from government, leaders in the nonprofit sector, for-profit sector, and civil society, it is feasible. It is also worth doing because the level of inefficiency fueled by mistrust in the current system is simply too great. The nonprofit sector and civil society cannot rise to meet the daunting challenges of the next seventy years without a new, more durable, and universal foundation for cooperation.

Conclusion

You might be wondering: Given all its problems, challenges, and inequities, is the nonprofit sector really worth nurturing? Wouldn't it be simpler to just let for-profit businesses take on these challenges? Or follow a European model where the government plays a much more active role in managing social programs and public goods?

I believe that a thriving nonprofit sector is worth the effort to nurture. Nonprofits are woven into our society and culture since the earliest days of this country. They have been, and continue to be, a source of support for people from all communities and backgrounds. At their best, they have the flexibility to drive innovation, have the nimbleness to be responsive to community needs, and are trustworthy vessels for our highest ideals. Every time someone chooses to donate time or money to a nonprofit, they are expressing the time-honored virtue of charity. Those gifts embody the original meaning of philanthropy, the love of humankind. I sincerely believe that building and sustaining a vibrant nonprofit sector in turn builds a healthy and compassionate society.

Nonprofits do face significant challenges, both internal and external. Trust in their ethics and competence has been in decline, and financial resources have remained stagnant. Competition for those resources is growing fiercer. The public policy landscape has often proven indifferent or even hostile to supporting financial stability or innovation at nonprofits. Internally, the sector has not proven immune from racism, sexism, ableism, or homophobia.

It is also true that in many respects, the sector has struggled to respond to those challenges. The challenge of stagnation has remained intractable for about forty years. Progress in making board leadership more diverse, inclusive, and equitable has been slow and uneven. Bad actors and scandals have continued to impact organizations of all sizes.

However, in the years and decades of struggle, the foundations upon which solutions to these problems can be built have been quietly assembled. The rise of big data and the associated push for transparency has created massive, public data sets that can be used to solve problems and build trust. The infrastructure of sophisticated communications created to serve an increasingly demanding donor base can help to develop relationships across sector boundaries. The development of accreditation systems to support specific parts of the sector, like healthcare and higher education, can be a blueprint for something sector wide.

Implementing these solutions will be a challenge that unfolds over years and decades and will only succeed with a lot of buy-in, generous investment, and some luck. But as an old boss of mine used to say, "If a goal doesn't scare you a little, is it really a goal?" I believe those investments will be worth it. The United States is entering a new and challenging era in its history. Faced with a shifting world order, an aging population, and wicked problems like climate change, it is more important than ever to have a thriving nonprofit sector. One that can build trust and strengthen the social fabric by supporting community-based, creative solutions and calling on each of us to listen to our better angels a little bit more.

I have spent all my adult life working and volunteering in nonprofits. In that time, I have seen plenty of things that are frustrating and flawed. But each day when I head to the office, I still feel the same urgency and intensity for transformation that inspired me on that gray January day where my career started. That is what *Amplifying Impact* is all about—betting on the potential and capacity of the nonprofit sector to help us build an equitable, sustainable, and inclusive future for all Americans.

Acknowledgments

Creating *Amplifying Impact* has truly been a labor of love. It would not have been possible without the generous advice, encouragement, and investment of so many people.

First, I would like to thank everyone who supported the book when it was just an idea:

Emily Shaw, Mark and Teresa Shrader, Kate and Meaghan Holcomb-Shrader, Leah Robbins Fowler, Allison McDade, Emily Holcomb, Robert Wiley, Agnieszka Kurzej, Christopher Monnette, Katherine Ettman, Anne Tengler, Annie Woodle, Eva Trust, Shawn O'Connor, Marissa Christie, Samantha Sgourakes, Valerie Greenhagen, Susan Sterne, Greg and Jennifer Holcomb, Ivy Higgins, Peter Sundry, Chris and Libby Marrs, William Drier, Evelyn Grace, and Eric Koester. This book would not be possible without your investment.

Second, I am sincerely grateful for the many colleagues, mentors, and experts in nonprofits who have supported me throughout my career: Alison Kolwaite, Paul Lanzone, Gayle

Geeter, Ashlei Watson, Shannon Corcoran, Sara Dougherty, Sarah Montgomery, Emmy Griffin, Mary Bridget Klinkerbergh, Melody Travis, Roxane White, and Benilda Samuels.

Finally, this book would not have been completed without the amazing teams at the Creator Institute and New Degree Press, particularly Kaity Van Riper, Erika Nichols-Frazer, and Shawna Quigley.

For everyone else who has supported me in creating this book who I have not mentioned by name, please accept my lasting gratitude.

Appendix

INTRODUCTION

Arnsberger, Paul, Melissa Ludlum, Margaret Riley, and Mark Stanton. U.S. Department of the Treasury. Internal Revenue Service. A History of the Tax-Exempt Sector: An SOI Perspective. Statistics of Income Bulletin. 2008. *https://www.irs.gov/pub/irs-soi/tehistory.pdf.*

Charity Navigator. "Giving Statistics." Accessed January 8, 2022. *https://www.charitynavigator.org/index.cfm?bay=content.view&cpid=42.*

Giving Institute, The. Giving USA 2020: Charitable giving showed solid growth, climbing to $449.64 billion in 2019, one of the highest years for giving on record. Accessed May 17, 2021. *https://givingusa.org/giving-usa-2020-charitable-giving-showed-solid-growth-climbing-to-449-64-billion-in-2019-one-of-the-highest-years-for-giving-on-record.*

Independent Sector. The Charitable Sector. Accessed May 17, 2021. *https://independentsector.org/about/the-charitable-sector.*

Salamon, Lester and Chelsea Newhouse. "The 2019 Nonprofit Employment Report." Nonprofit Economic Bulletin No. 47. (January 2019): 1–17. *http://ccss.jhu.edu/wp-content/uploads/downloads/2019/01/2019-NP-Employment-Report_FINAL_1.8.2019.pdf.*

CHAPTER 1: HOW DID WE GET HERE? NONPROFIT HISTORY

Arnsberger, Paul, Melissa Ludlum, Margaret Riley, and Mark Stanton. U.S. Department of the Treasury. Internal Revenue Service. A History of the Tax-Exempt Sector: An SOI Perspective. Statistics of Income Bulletin. 2008. *https://www.irs.gov/pub/irs-soi/tehistory.pdf.*

An Act to reduce taxation, to provide revenue for the Government, and for other purposes. Public Law 53-349, US Statutes at Large 28 (1894): 509–571. *https://fraser.stlouisfed.org/title/tariff-1894-wilson-gorman-tariff-5901/fulltext.*

Carlson, L. Gregg. "Perspectives on ** Giving USA 2014 ** from the Chair of the Giving USA Foundation." Insights from the Giving Institute (blog). November 30, 2014. *https://givingusa.org/perspectives-on-giving-usa-2014-from-the-chair-of-the-giving-usa-foundation.*

Milward, H. Brinton and Keith Provan. "Governing the Hollow State." Journal of Public Administration Research and Theory, Volume 10, Issue 2 (2000). *https://doi.org/10.1093/oxfordjournals.jpart.a024273.*

Rada, James. Battlefield Angels: The Daughters of Charity Work as Civil War Nurses. Pacific Grove: Smashwords, 2014.

The Revenue Act of 1917. United States Statutes at Large 300. 1917. *https://www.law.cornell.edu/topn/revenue_act_of_1917.*

CHAPTER 2: FOLLOW THE MONEY: HOW NONPROFIT FUNDING PRACTICES SHAPE THE SECTOR

Blau, Reuven. "Struggling Nonprofits Urge Mayor de Blasio to Speed Up Late Payments." The City. May 19, 2019. *https://www.thecity.nyc/government/2019/5/22/21211064/struggling-nonprofits-urge-mayor-de-blasio-to-speed-up-late-payments.*

Browning, Jessica. "Trends That Will Shape Philanthropy in 2022." Insights from the Giving Institute (blog). December 16, 2021. *https://givingusa.org/trends-that-will-shape-philanthropy-in-2022.*

Colorado Symphony. Giving. Accessed June 15, 2022. *https://coloradosymphony.org/Giving.*

Corporate Finance Institute. Endowment Fund: An Investment Portfolio with the Initial Capital Coming from Donations. 2022. *https://givingusa.org/trends-that-will-shape-philanthropy-in-2022.*

Drees, Jackie. "12 EHR Implementations That Cost Over $100M." Becker's Health IT. February 25, 2020. *https://www.beckershospitalreview.com/ehrs/12-ehr-implementations-that-cost-over-100m.html.*

Hoffower, Hillary and Dominic-Madori Davis. "The Party of the Year for the Fashion World Was Scheduled to Take Place Today. From $30,000 Tickets to $2,000 Tuxedos, Take a Look at Just How Opulent the Met Gala Usually Is." Business Insider, May 4, 2020. *https://www.businessinsider.com/met-gala-2018-theme-cost-ticket-dress-jewlery-2018-5#it-reportedly-cost-35-million-to-produce-the-met-gala-in-2016-1.*

PND. "What Does the Nonprofit Sector Really Look Like?" Candid Blog (blog). October 22, 2021. *https://trust.guidestar.org/what-does-the-nonprofit-sector-really-look-like.*

Le, Vu. "We Need to Rethink the Idea of Diversified Funding." Nonprofit AF (blog). April 4, 2021. *https://nonprofitaf.com/2021/04/we-need-to-rethink-the-idea-of-diversified-funding/#more-7206.*

Tseng, P., R.S. Kaplan, B.D. Richman, M.A. Shah, and K.A. Schulman. Administrative Costs Associated with Physician Billing and Insurance-Related Activities at an Academic Health Care System. JAMA. 2018. doi:10.1001/jama.2017.19148

Urban Institute, The: National Center for Charitable Statistics. The Nonprofit Sector in Brief. 2022. *https://nccs.urban.org/project/nonprofit-sector-brief.*

U.S. Department of the Treasury, Internal Revenue Service. Publication 598: Tax on Unrelated Business Income of Exempt Organizations. Washington, DC: GPO 2021. *https://www.irs.gov/pub/irs-pdf/p598.pdf.*

Young, Shannon. "Nonprofits Press Cuomo, Lawmakers to End Contract Payment Delays." Politico. August 3, 2020. *https://*

humanservicescouncil.org/wp-content/uploads/2020/08/Nonprofits-press-Cuomo-lawmakers-to-end-contract-payment-delays-8.3.20.pdf.

CHAPTER 3: TRUST: IT'S COMPLICATED

Bryce, Herrington. Players in the Public Policy Process: Nonprofits as Social Capital and Agents. New York: Palgrave Macmillan, 2005.

Bryce, Herrington. "The Public's Trust in Nonprofit Organizations: The Role of Relationship Marketing and Management." The Nonprofit Quarterly. January 11, 2016. *https://nonprofitquarterly.org/the-publics-trust-in-nonprofit-organizations-the-role-of-relationship-marketing-and-management.*

Daniel J. Edelman Holdings. Edelman Trust Barometer 2021. January 12, 2022. *https://www.edelman.com/sites/g/files/aatuss191/files/2021-03/2021%20Edelman%20Trust%20Barometer.pdf.*

Independent Sector. Trust in Civil Society: Understanding the Factors Driving Trust in Nonprofits and Philanthropy. Accessed July 20, 2021. *https://independentsector.org/news-post/independent-sector-releases-second-annual-report-on-trust-in-civil-society.*

CHAPTER 4: HIGH STAKES PHILANTHROPY: THE RISKS AND REWARDS OF MASSIVE GIFTS

Association of Fundraising Professionals. "Fundraising Effectiveness Project: Giving Increases Significantly in 2020, Even as Donor Retention Rates Shrink." March 15, 2021. *https://*

afpglobal.org/fundraising-effectiveness-project-giving-increases-significantly-2020-even-donor-retention-rates.

Axelrad, Claire. "How to Measure Donor Acquisition Costs." Ask An Expert (blog). Accessed December 5, 2021. *https://bloomerang.co/blog/ask-an-expert-how-to-measure-donor-acquisition-costs.*

Bill & Melinda Gates Foundation, The. "Foundation Commits $335 Million to Promote Effective Teaching and Raise Student Achievement." Press Release. The Bill & Melinda Gates Foundation website. Accessed July 14, 2021. *https://www.gatesfoundation.org/ideas/media-center/press-releases/2009/11/foundation-commits-$335-million-to-promote-effective-teaching-and-raise-student-achievement.*

Di Mento, Maria. "The Philanthropy 50." The Chronicle of Philanthropy. February 8, 2022. *https://www.philanthropy.com/article/the-philanthropy-50/?cid=gen_sign_in#id=browse_2021.*

Finkelstein, James and Judith Wilde. "Bonuses and Benefits." Inside Higher Education. May 25, 2017. https://www.insidehighered.com/advice/2017/05/25/examination-growing-number-perks-and-bonuses-college-presidents-essay.

Greene, Jay. "The Gates Effective Teaching Initiative Fails to Improve Student Outcomes." Education Next (blog). June 22, 2018. https://www.educationnext.org/gates-effective-teaching-initiative-fails-improve-student-outcomes.

Hadero, Haleluya. "Charitable Giving in the U.S. Reaches All-time High in 2020." The Associated Press. June 15, 2021.

Accessed October 25, 2021. *https://apnews.com/article/philanthropy-health-coronavirus-pandemic-business-94cac51d5caf-18f48a7827de04e017c0.*

Lilly Family School of Philanthropy, The. "Changes to the Giving Landscape." 2019. *https://scholarworks.iupui.edu/bitstream/handle/1805/21217/vanguard-charitable191022.pdf?sequence=1&isAllowed=y.*

Statista. "Millionaires in the United States–Statistics and Facts. 2022. *https://www.statista.com/topics/3467/millionaires-in-the-united-states/#dossierKeyfigures.*

Stecher, Brian M., Deborah J. Holtzman, Michael S. Garet, Laura S. Hamilton, John Engberg, Elizabeth D. Steiner, Abby Robyn, Matthew D. Baird, Italo A. Gutierrez, Evan D. Peet, et al. "Improving Teaching Effectiveness. Final Report: The Intensive Partnerships for Effective Teaching Through 2015–2016." Santa Monica, CA: RAND Corporation, 2018. *https://www.rand.org/pubs/research_reports/RR2242.html.*

Urban Institute, The. National Center for Charitable Statistics. "The Nonprofit Sector in Brief." 2022. *https://nccs.urban.org/project/nonprofit-sector-brief.*

CHAPTER 5: INCLUSION AND INCENTIVES: THE POWER OF NONPROFIT BOARDS

BoardSource. "Leading With Intent: Reviewing the State of Diversity Equity and Inclusion on Nonprofit Boards." June 2021. *https://leadingwithintent.org/diversity-equity-and-inclu-*

sion-findings/?utm_referrer=https percent3A percent2F percent-2Fleadingwithintent.org percent2F.

BoardSource. "Recommended Governance Practices." 2022. https://boardsource.org/wp-content/uploads/2016/10/Recommended-Gov-Practices.pdf.

Foundation Group. What is a 501(c)(3)? website. Accessed November 19, 2021. https://www.501c3.org/what-is-a-501c3.

Funders for LGBTQ Issues. "The Philanthropic Closet: LGBTQ People in Philanthropy." October 2018. https://lgbtfunders.org/wp-content/uploads/2018/02/The_Philanthropic_Closet_2018_Full.pdf.

Haughey, John. "House Panel Grills Domestic Violence Nonprofit Board Members Over Nonprofit's CEO Compensation." The Center Square Florida, February 25, 2020. https://www.thecentersquare.com/florida/house-panel-grills-domestic-violence-board-members-over-nonprofit-s-ceo-compensation/article_1aaedfde-57df-11ea-9a2d-6b4822e48767.html.

Independent Sector. "Trust in Civil Society: Understanding the Factors Driving Trust in Nonprofits and Philanthropy." June 1, 2020. https://independentsector.org/wp-content/uploads/2020/06/Trust-in-Civil-Society-62420.pdf.

Lilly Family School of Philanthropy, The. "The Impact of Diversity: Understanding How Nonprofit Board Diversity Affects Philanthropy, Leadership, and Board Engagement." February 2018. https://scholarworks.iupui.edu/bitstream/handle/1805/15239/board-diversity180220.pdf?sequence=1&isAllowed=y.

Long, Marjorie. Fundamentals of Nonprofit Best Legal Practices. Highlands Ranch: EdLex Resources, 2018.

National Council of Nonprofits. Board Roles and Responsibilities. 2022. *https://www.councilofnonprofits.org/tools-resources/board-roles-and-responsibilities.*

Paynter, Ben. "Nonprofit Boards Are Very Rich and Very White." Fast Company, September 6, 2017. *https://www.fastcompany.com/40462347/nonprofits-boards-are-very-rich-and-very-white.*

Reeves, Megan. "Florida Nonprofit's Misspending Trickled Down into Tampa Bay's Domestic Violence Shelters." Tampa Bay Times. March 4, 2020. *https://www.tampabay.com/florida-politics/buzz/2020/03/04/florida-nonprofits-misspending-trickled-down-into-tampa-bays-domestic-violence-shelters.*

Schwartz, Robert, James Weinberg, Dana Hagenbuch, and Allison Scott. "The Voice of Nonprofit Talent: Perceptions of Diversity in the Workplace." Boston: Common Good Careers, 2015. *https://www.smash.org/wp-content/uploads/2015/05/voice_of_nonprofit_talent.pdf.*

U.S. Census Bureau. Quick Facts United States: What's New. Washington, DC: 2022. *https://www.census.gov/quickfacts/fact/table/US/RHI125219.*

CHAPTER 6: NONPROFITS AND GOVERNMENT FROM PASSIVE TO PARTNERS

An Act To provide for Reconciliation Pursuant to Titles II and V of the Concurrent Resolution on the Budget for Fiscal Year 2018. Public Law 115-97 U.S. Statutes At Large 121 (2017).

Curtis, Keith. "Decoding Donor-Advised Funs from Data to Day to Day." Giving USA Insights (blog). February 3, 2022. *https:// givingusa.org/decoding-donor-advised-funds-from-data-to-day-to-day.*

Giving USA. "Giving USA 2020: Charitable Giving Showed Solid Growth, Climbing to $449.64 billion in 2019, One of the Highest Years for Giving on Record." Press Release, June 16, 2020. Accessed July 17, 2021. *https://givingusa.org/giving-usa-2020-charitable-giving-showed-solid-growth-climbing-to-449-64-billion-in-2019-one-of-the-highest-years-for-giving-on-record.*

Markowitz, Andy. "Late Payments to Nonprofits in Ill. Become Routine." The Chronicle of Philanthropy. October 20, 2011. *https://www.philanthropy.com/article/late-payments-to-nonprofits-in-ill-become-routine.*

Milward, H. Brinton. Review of Nonprofit Contracting and the Hollow State, by Susan R. Bernstein, Steven Rathgeb Smith, Michael Lipsky, and Jennifer Wolch. Public Administration Review 54, no. 1 (1994). *https://doi.org/10.2307/976501.*

National Philanthropic Trust, The. The 2021 DAF Report. 2022. Accessed January 18, 2022. *https://www.nptrust.org/reports/daf-report.*

Pension Protection Act of 2006, 29 USC 1001 Sect. 1 et seq. *https://www.govinfo.gov/content/pkg/PLAW-109publ280/pdf/PLAW-109publ280.pdf.*

Salamon, Lester and Chelsea Newhouse. "The 2019 Nonprofit Employment Report." Nonprofit Economic Bulletin No. 47. January 2019. *http://ccss.jhu.edu/wp-content/uploads/downloads/2019/01/2019-NP-Employment-Report_FINAL_1.8.2019.pdf.*

U.S. Department of the Treasury. Internal Revenue Service. Instructions for Form 990 Return of Organization Exempt from Income Tax (2021). Washington, DC: GPO 2021. Accessed January 19, 2022. *https://www.irs.gov/instructions/i990.*

CHAPTER 7: THE SPECIAL RELATIONSHIP: CONNECTIONS BETWEEN DONORS AND NONPROFITS

Campbell, Joseph. The Hero with A Thousand Faces. 3rd Ed. New York: Pantheon, 2008.

Charity Navigator. "Financial Score Conversions and Tables." 2022. *https://www.charitynavigator.org/index.cfmbay=content.view&cpid=48#PerformanceMetricFour.*

CHAPTER 8: TRUST BUT VERIFY: A CASE FOR A NONPROFIT ACCREDITATION MODEL

Institute of Medicine (US) Committee on Assessing the System for Protecting Human Research Subjects. Preserving Public Trust: Accreditation and Human Research Participant Protection

Programs. Washington, DC: National Academies Press, 2001. https://www.ncbi.nlm.nih.gov/books/NBK43599.

Joint Commission, The. "Facts about the Joint Commission." 2022. https://www.jointcommission.org/about-us/facts-about-the-joint-commission.

The Oxford English Dictionary Online. s.v. "accreditation." Accessed August 19, 2021. https://www.oed.com.

Urban Institute, The. "National Center for Charitable Statistics. The Nonprofit Sector in Brief." 2022. https://nccs.urban.org/project/nonprofit-sector-brief.

CHAPTER 9: ELEMENTS OF A SECTOR-WIDE ACCREDITATION SYSTEM

Akerlof, George. The Market for Lemons: Quality, Uncertainty and the Market Mechanism. New York: Academic Press, 1978. https://doi.org/10.1016/B978-0-12-214850-7.50022-X.

Bearman, Jessica. "Grant Reporting: The Current State of Practice." Peak Grantmaking Insights (blog). January 22, 2018. https://www.peakgrantmaking.org/insights/grant-reporting-the-current-state-of-practice.

Karlan, Dean and John List. "How Can Bill and Melinda Gates Increase Other People's Donations to Fund Public Goods?" NBER Working Paper No. 17954, March 2012. Revised August 2020. https://www.nber.org/system/files/working_papers/w17954/w17954.pdf.

Middle States Commission on Higher Education. "Accreditation Standards." 2022. *https://www.msche.org/standards/#standard_2.*

Middle States Commission on Higher Education. "Institution Directory." 2022. *https://www.msche.org/institution/0126.*

O'Hare, Paul, Iain White, Angela Connelly. "Insurance as Maladaptation: Resilience and the 'Business as Usual' Paradox." *(https://www.research.manchester.ac.uk/portal/en/publications/insurance-as-maladaptation-resilience-and-the-business-as-usual-paradox(ac6977b8-52f0-4c9f-a213-466296b14220).html).* Environment and Planning C: Government and Policy, Sep 2015. *https://doi.org/10.1177/0263774X15602022.*

Urban Institute, The. "National Center for Charitable Statistics. The Nonprofit Sector in Brief." 2022. *https://nccs.urban.org/project/nonprofit-sector-brief.*

CHAPTER 10: PUTTING ACCREDITATION INTO PRACTICE

Association for the Accreditation of Human Research Protection Programs. "About AAHRPP." 2022. *https://www.aahrpp.org/learn/about-aahrpp/our-mission.*

Carman, Joanne and Kimberly Fredericks. "Nonprofits and Accreditation: Exploring the Implications for Accountability." International Review of Public Administration. March 2014. 18(3) 51-68 DOI:10.1080/12294659.2013.10805263.

Electronic Healthcare Network Accreditation Commission. "EHNAC Overview." 2022. *https://www.ehnac.org/about.*

Watts, Duncan. Understanding US/UK Government and Politics. Manchester: Manchester University Press, 2003.

www.ingramcontent.com/pod-product-compliance
Lightning Source LLC
LaVergne TN
LVHW012019060526
838201LV00061B/4372